MW01672719

INVISIBLE FAMILIES

for

PARENTS OF LESBIAN AND GAY CHILDREN

Terry Stewart

Heartflags Publishing

The Author

Terry Stewart is the mother of two sons, the elder of whom is gay. A church-going parent who signed the petition against the Homosexual Law Reform Bill in 1985, she shares the information and insights gained on her own journey of discovery.

Terry was born in England and moved to New Zealand in 1952, marrying Ron, a dairy farmer, in 1965. Active in church and community affairs for many years, she holds a tertiary certificate in Caring Education based on community care for the disabled and mentally ill and has worked as a liaison officer for the Northland Mental Health Association (now Trust).

First published as *Invisible Families: a New Zealand Resource for Parents of Lesbian and Gay Children* in 1993 by New Women's Press
Reprinted in 1994
Revised and updated in 1996 by Tandem Press
Revised 2011 by Heartflags Publishing
This edition and cover design by Heartflags Publishing

ISBN 978-0-9805523-0-0

National Library of Australia Cataloguing-in-Publication entry

Author:	Stewart, Terry, 1938-
Title:	Invisible Families: for parents of lesbian and gay children / Terry Stewart.
ISBN:	9780980552300 (pbk.)
Notes:	Bibliography.
Subjects:	Gays--Family relationships. Parents of gays. Lesbians--Family relationships.
Dewey Number:	306.766

Contents

This book is dedicated with love to our son; and to all those daughters and sons who are lesbian, gay, or bisexual.

Acknowledgements

Writing this book has been for me a deeply emotional learning experience. In seeking information, I was referred to others, had books recommended to me or was supplied with more articles and pamphlets — in fact such a sense of rightness developed about the whole project that as I formed questions answers seemed to 'magically' arrive — giving me a much needed confidence and support, particularly in those first early months.

I am most grateful to every person who wrote letters and/or filled in questionnaires. Each of you gave so much. You have made these pages come alive. You shared your love, joy and/or pain with me — a stranger. It was humbling and underlined my at times heavily felt responsibility. When you told me of your anguish for dearly loved sons, family members, or friends who had an HIV infection, or who had died from AIDS, I grieved with you.

Especially my thanks are due to: Kevin Hague (New Zealand AIDS Foundation Auckland), Phil Parkinson (Lesbian & Gay Archives of New Zealand, Wellington), Jenny Rankine (NZAF Auckland), Alison Laurie (Victoria University of Wellington), Barry Taylor (then with Ministry of Youth Affairs, Wellington), Cathie Dunsford (Dunsford & Associates), and Karl Pulotu-Endemann (Pacific Islands AIDS Trust), without whose expertise, generous support and continued encouragement over the last two and a half years my task would have at many times threatened to overwhelm me.

I wish to acknowledge the work of the NSW Anti-Discrimination Board, whose report was the only antipodean resource I found which covered so many of the issues surrounding the subject. It inspired much of my own research and provided material I was able to use extensively.

My grateful thanks for their support, encouragement and in many cases personal contributions to: Tony Hughes, Leigh Rampton and other staff NZAF, Auckland; Keith Stuart and staff of the Burnett Centre; Trish Gribben; Roger Swanson and Glenda Gale, LAGA, Wellington; Sally Liggins and Jenni Tarrant, NZ Family Planning Association; Ngahuia Te Awekotuku, University of Auckland; Felix Donnelly, Youth Link Trust, Auckland; Deirdre Milne, Milne, Ireland & Walker, Auckland; Bill Logan; Hugh Young; Ann-Marie Stapp; Julie Helean, then with Isherwood Trust, Auckland; Chris Farrelly, AIDS Coordinator, and Trish Holloway, HP Unit, Northland Area Health Board; The Rt Rev. Bruce Gilberd, Anglican Bishop of Auckland; The Rt Rev. John Murray, former Moderator of the Presbyterian Church in New Zealand; the Rev. Geoffrey Vine; Max Abbott, Barbara Disley and Dell Coyte, Mental Health Foundation of NZ; Heather Came; Ilene Wilson; Wayne Mullineaux; Jo Crowley; Susan Hukui, TVNZ; Helen Packard, HELP Foundation, Auckland; Stephen Jacobs; Ian Kember and the Gay Broadcast Collective, Wellington; Maggie Barry, then with Radio NZ; Melanie Jones and Jenni Austin, NZ Woman's Weekly; and the ever helpful reference librarians at the Whangarei Public Library.

Sincere thanks to those individual members within the following groups who supported my work and research: Northland Area Gay Support Group; Northland Lesbian Support Network; Northland AIDS Support Network; Lifeline, Whangarei; Parent Help and Youth Help, Whangarei; Awhina Centre, Wellington; Spectrum, Nelson; Lambda Centre, Christchurch; Auckland Lesbian & Gay Youth Group; Aoraki Lesbian & Gay Group, Temuka; Auckland Gay-Lesbian Welfare Group Inc.; Gay Auckland Business Association; the Metropolitan Community Churches; the reconciliation support groups of the Presbyterian, Methodist, Anglican and Catholic churches, and the Religious Society of Friends (Quakers); Radio GALA Auckland; and Parents of Lesbians, Gays & Bisexuals NZ (Auckland) Inc. If I have missed any group, please forgive me — you know who you are.

Special thanks are due to Jae Oldbury and Margaret Murray, for their friendship and help, together with the Executive Committee of the Northland Mental Health Trust for their sponsorship, support and personal encouragement.

Without the unflagging belief in the project by my husband Ron (who also supplied endless cups of tea!), my son and his partner, my younger son and all members of our family who endured my obsessiveness for months on end, the book would not have been completed — to you all, my loving thanks.

To my friends Penny K, Jewel H., and Liz M., for providing perspective, and always being there for me when needed — thank you.

Finally and most importantly to my talented publisher Wendy Harrex, without whose inspiration, encouragement and editing expertise the book would not have become a reality, on behalf of our own and all of New Zealand's 'Invisible Families' — my sincere and grateful thanks.

Thankyou Mum

I want to apologise for any problems
that I may have caused you in the past
I am not the easiest person to live with
since I am so independent and strong
but you can be sure
that though it possibly didn't seem like it
your values and ideals did pass on to me
and I carry them forward in all that I do
You were always someone
stable, strong, giving and warm
an ideal person to look up to
this has given me the strength to lead
my own life
according to my own standards
Your leadership and love have enabled me to grow
into a very happy person and I think that is
what every mother wishes
for her child.
Thankyou.

This poem by Susan Polls Schutz was sent to me by a mother whose son gave it to her on leaving home to live with his partner. Reproduced with permission.

Our Own Story

In 1987 our eldest son, who was boarding elsewhere in Whangarei, asked if he and a male friend could come home to live, as their landlady could no longer have them due to a change in her personal circumstances. We happily agreed.

After two months it slowly dawned on us that this might be more than a friendship; this could in fact be a relationship! Their behaviour did not obviously indicate that this was so, but small signs had gradually added up to a suspicion.

We were astounded and somewhat shocked. Naively we knew very little about homosexuality. Our son and his friend were not in any way stereotypical of what we somewhat vaguely, and certainly negatively, had assumed gay men to be. In hindsight we did recall a few isolated incidents with our son which had puzzled us. Now strung together, these began to make a kind of sense, which then we would rather not have acknowledged. Meanwhile, for two long months, we watched them surreptitiously for any confirmation that we were right! Their deception, sadly well learnt, was masterly.

We thought they might tell us themselves if we waited. However, they then made plans for leaving us to live in a major city. We were in turmoil. If we let them go without broaching the issue, we reasoned there might never be the same opportunity again to ask them if we were right. They would go away, form a new life and perhaps become estranged from us. Might we even gradually lose contact with our son?

Eventually our need to know overcame our fear that, should we be wrong, he could be extremely offended. When, after my questioning, he said, 'Yes, I am gay, and yes, this is a relationship,' it was a relief. It explained much about his attitudes and unsettled life of the past four years, when at times our normally excellent relationship with him had become tense and unhappy. Relief was fleeting, for it quickly turned to deepest grief and later to burning anger, when we discovered what hurt and rejection he had experienced over this time.

Away at boarding school for his final year, to ease we hoped the transition from a smaller high school to university, he had discovered his homosexuality and been mercilessly victimised by his peers. Being strong of character he stood his ground, which served to provoke the bullies further. The physical and other harassment he had endured caused us to rethink the entire meaning of the word 'perverted'.

Raised in a family where church beliefs and values were important, he assumed and feared that we would react strongly and negatively. Certainly we were conservative people. In the past, trying to be open-minded, we had believed that to be gay was 'unfortunate' at best. We were mortified to recall that we had signed a church petition against the Homosexual Law Reform Bill and that our son knew of this.

This book is in part our attempt at reparation, as we regret that action deeply. We feel there could be many church members and other caring people who, like ourselves, may have acted similarly from a lack of knowledge and understanding.

Unfortunately at this crucial time I was unwell, recovering from major surgery that had prolonged complications. As a result, our son had doubly felt he could not tell us what was wrong, even when we asked, for we were by then aware he was unhappy.

Desperately he had felt our love and respect was the one stable point in his existence and could not be risked. We learnt he had been to a local church for support and had been told he was 'abominable and perverted'. His own sense of self-worth said this was not so, but eventually the months of stress culminated in an attempted suicide, about which the school had not informed us. We were utterly appalled.

There had followed a difficult period for us all. Having sufficient savings, fourteen months later he went to Australia. Although not happy about this, for we were by now frequently troubled and extremely worried, we felt powerless to stop him. His two years in Australia were both good and at times depressingly hard for him. Now he told us that at this point he had for a while turned to street drugs in an effort to dull the pain (see also Chapter 9).

Steadfastly he had refused to confide what was wrong. These revelations shocked us terribly. Afraid for him, we grieved, feeling we had failed him.

So, loved and accepted, he and his partner now went away as planned. Immersed in their own private world they did not realise we were seething with unasked questions and needing information. Nor that we were beginning a process which would take us a long time, as they had taken time, to come fully to terms with the wide spectrum of issues relating to homosexuality.

Certainly our sons were not deprived of our attention. Raised on a dairy farm they had ongoing, affectionate interaction with us both. When they were older Ron took them fishing, camping and possum hunting. We both fostered their education and after-school activities. They often visited both sets of fond grandparents.

Ron is a caring and loving father. By nature he is calm and pragmatic, so, while not fully understanding, he could accept that if his son said he was gay, then this was so. He believed his son, a young man with a strong personality, would not have deliberately 'chosen' to be gay and voluntarily be so badly hurt and rejected. He thought we had been adequate parents and were not the 'cause'. He did blame himself for not encouraging him to talk more when recognising something was wrong. Believing any problems to be a case of 'teenage blues', he had not interfered, hoping for a natural resolution with time.

While totally accepting my son, I reacted differently. Feeling that I was perhaps the parent with more influence on his developmental years, maybe somehow it was my fault he was gay?

I worried about vaguely remembered psychologically

based misinformation and cried from feelings of ambivalence and deep distress. Eventually I spoke to colleagues, many of whom were social workers; they listened kindly, but had little real knowledge to offer. 'Accept what is' was their advice. This made me frustrated and irritable! I needed proper information from which to work through my feelings of grief, guilt and fear. At that time the local library had no recent books on the subject. Those available were outdated, from the 1960s and early 1970s and many had been defaced or had pages removed. These just confused me further.

As time went on I finally became brave enough to search the sections on homosexuality in the bigger city bookstores. I was directed to the recognised classic, *Loving Someone Gay* by Don Clark (now republished as *The New Loving Someone Gay*). Excellent as the book was, the author was himself gay, and therefore 'biased' in my uninformed eyes, and culturally it was American — but it helped. Later I came across an article by Dr Max Abbott, then Director of the Mental Health Foundation of New Zealand, called 'Homosexuality — An overview of research and professional opinion', which was the text of a public address he had given in Lower Hutt in 1985. This was better; we could both accept this as an unbiased opinion by a local man, who was respected both personally and in his field of work.

By the late 1980s several books written for parents, by parents of lesbian daughters or gay sons, were available in some specialty bookstores. Being imported, these tended to be expensive. We wished there was something written for New Zealand parents that was more appropriate to our needs but could find nothing.

Today, as a result of my reading and reflection, I understand that my reaction was shaped by the messages I had received in my own upbringing. As the eldest of three children I had become through a variety of circumstances an archetypal 'good girl', like many of my generation. It seemed in retrospect I had unconsciously felt that I could never quite measure up to the standards required at home, school or church. I did however achieve a guilt complex, which I pursued into adulthood by imposing upon myself my well learnt perfectionist standards. Like many mothers, conditioned by a myth of 'perfect motherhood', I tended to blame myself. My son's homosexuality was, like everything else, somehow my fault!

It is comparatively recently, through talking with a community psychologist, that this insight of imposed guilt has become clear I said 'Right, I don't need this' and mentally threw it out! The freedom was magical, for the accumulated burden of some forty-five years rolled away! This imposed guilt may apply particularly to mothers. We all as parents need to remember that we have done the best we were able at any given point in time.

In January 1991, while attending a writing course tutored by Dr Cathie Dunsford, I was introduced to publisher Wendy Harrex of New Women's Press, who challenged me to write a resource for other parents of lesbian or gay children. A few weeks later I submitted a synopsis of what I felt such a book might contain.

Not daring to expect this would be accepted, I went ahead with plans to do a full-time course in journalism.

When Wendy offered me a contract, I panicked! What had I done? Could I pass up this opportunity when I knew such a book was needed? After discussing it with Ron, our sons, Cathie and others, with great trepidation I decided to at least give it a try.

Realising I had to access parents, other family members and lesbian, gay or bisexual women and men themselves, I decided to advertise, to go public. This was truly frightening! It was my own 'coming out' — the point of personal recognition that from here on there would be no possibility of withdrawing from the commitment.

With our son's permission, other family members were informed. They said, 'He is one of us, we love him, even if we do not fully understand.' For us, it was good to stop prevaricating about his relationship and other matters. I found that my sisters had guessed, thinking he had been expelled from school because he was gay. This was not so, the decision to leave was his, although forced by his unhappiness.

In the time prior to an article being published in the New Zealand Woman's Weekly and before I was to be interviewed on National Radio, I experienced bouts of insomnia and agitation; paranoia gripped me! Sternly, I told myself, 'Think how it feels to be a teenager facing coming out to their family and others.'

Happily, among the letters I subsequently received, only four were in any way contentious. (One person assured me that 'they' can be 'cured' by a good diet and herbs. I could not resist wondering if such a diet had affected her own sexuality?)

Since then it has been my privilege to meet parents who were able to accept their daughters' and sons' different sexuality with no problems at all; wonderful mothers who spoke out on television after their sons died from AIDS; other parents who were running support groups; and those who had defended their children's rights at the time of the Reform Bill. We have a further common bond — we are dismayed and angry at the injustices, myths, bigotry, misinformation and prejudice which put our children — and still puts the lives of other young New Zealanders — in jeopardy.

Thousands of lesbian, gay and bisexual people in our community have not been given due recognition largely because parents, family and friends have been kept in ignorance, have assimilated the prevailing homophobia, believed the myths or misinformation fed to them, and been unaware of new knowledge and insights.

It appears that some political, church and business bases have vested interests, either in power dominance or financially, in keeping homosexuals 'ghettoised'. Unwittingly many parents, family and friends of lesbians and gay men support these interests by default, in not questioning fully the motives behind the information they supply.

Ron and I have discovered, as have many others, that positive information is available — although it is somewhat difficult to find, particularly if one does not live in or near a major city. In the following pages I will take you on a speeded-up journey of discovery which follows our own, but which took us four years!

Why This Book Was Written

As parents, we unwittingly internalise and assume strong heterosexual expectations for our children. Generally the ideal of caring parental love equates with the desire that our children will all marry, have 2.4 offspring and be financially successful — this, of course, will ensure their future happiness! We will then be personally validated and recognised by our peers as 'good' parents.

The day we discover or finally have confirmed to us that our child is lesbian, gay or bisexual affects us deeply. This reaction is to some extent governed by the emotional messages and information we have absorbed, by what standards we were raised to accept, and by how we have perceived sexuality: in other words, by what we have learnt to be 'good', 'bad', or 'normal'. My husband Ron says, 'Information gives power. Many people do not think things right through. The resultant situation is they are half-informed or misinformed — and feel let down, confused and powerless.'

There are many complex issues surrounding homosexuality. I may not supply answers to all your questions, but it is hoped this book will stimulate a need to know, providing a starting-point for further research should it be necessary. I hope that it will aid your family and others in talking openly about homosexuality, help in healing any rifts, and assist in a loving understanding of your lesbian, gay or bisexual daughters, sons or family members.

By reading of the experiences of other families and using the resources on coping (Chapter 12), may it be easier for you than it was for our son, his partner, and for us.

Above all, I want the despair and depression felt by daughters and sons due to the pressures of homophobia to be lessened; and should any suicides or attempted suicides be prevented, this collective effort will have been amply repaid. It cannot be said too strongly or too often, that the rejection felt by those who are lesbian or gay rates as a major cause of death for many of our young, and not so young, New Zealanders.

It is my dream today that soon parents will feel able to allow their lesbian and gay young people to investigate their sexuality from the shelter of their own home, as of right, as do their heterosexual brothers and sisters. With deep regret I feel that we let our son down in this regard by not being more aware of his needs and situation. When lesbian or gay teenagers are allowed to mix socially with like friends they will not feel compelled to leave home too young, nor will they in doing so seek to 'find' themselves by experiencing unwise or detrimental sexual liaisons. Instead, they will become well-balanced people having learnt happily and without disapproval that it is okay to be themselves.

This is for parents a whole new experience. Says one mother, 'I have to smile when I see my seventeen year old son and nineteen year old daughter both noticing with approval the same male jogging past the house.' She is in a hard-won place of total nderstanding. It has to be admitted this scenario would freak out most of us, particularly when newly aware of our child's homosexuality.

Total understanding is not only loving the person, it recognises their sexuality as an indivisible part of their whole being. Indeed it goes beyond even this, for it embraces a proactive position, which when possible seeks to inform others and does not allow them to discriminate against our beloved daughters and sons. This can only be achieved from a position of power — and information is power. I hope this book will empower you and your loved ones.

From personal experience Ron and I can now say: 'Yes, coming out, whether as parents or as daughters and sons, is hard — the obstacles may seem too steep — but we can assure you that once you are over the largely self-inflicted barricade any problems on the other side are not so great. It is essential to organise a back-up of good personal support first, but it can and will be fulfilling and liberating.' I encourage you to be brave, proud, and stand tall!

TERRY STEWART June 1993

Sexuality is not Just "part of my life" it is my whole being. Sexuality should be incorporated in every aspect such as spirituality or values

Saying that my sexuality is only a part of me
That there is so much more is heteronormative
By categorizing this, one is not fully encorporating
it into their lives thus never really becoming
whole. "This part of me may be wrong but
I have this otherside that is normative." wrong

Words and Their Meanings

The terms used to describe sexual expression and the ideas of homosexuality and heterosexuality have changed according to the culture of the times. Words may also have different meanings depending on who is using them. Some of the most important terms are described here, while others are included in a glossary at the end of the book.

Homosexual: This refers to both men and women unless I have used the individual terms 'lesbian' or 'gay man'.

Gay: In the past, this word has been used for both men and women, but it is now mainly used by gay men, though some women do use the term. It has been used in New Zealand since the early 1970s and mainly recognises a particular male homosexual identity and the sub-culture which has evolved in association with this identity.

It is essential to recognise the difference between:

Sexual Orientation: I have used this term to mean the direction of a person's sexual interest. Both men and women may have a sexual orientation towards people of their own gender, people of the opposite gender, or to people of either gender. Thus a man may be a homosexual, a heterosexual, or a bisexual in orientation, and a woman may be a lesbian, a heterosexual, or a bisexual in orientation. (As will be seen, sexual orientation is believed to be established very early in life.)

Sexual Identity: I have used this term to mean how people self-disclose and represent their sexuality, both to themselves and to other people. In the case of homosexual and bisexual men or lesbian and bisexual women, who at first identified as heterosexual, this is often because the person has not yet realised what their sexual orientation is, or has not yet come to terms with it. A person's sexual identity is something which reflects their orientation or which (in some cases) is adopted or chosen. It is a social label or category.

Sexual Behaviour: Although a person's sexual behaviour usually coincides with their sexual orientation and identity, this is not always the case. For example, a man with heterosexual orientation and identity may have had a sexual liaison with another man at some time or another. I have found that sexual behaviour is believed by many people to be synonymous with orientation, which is not always the case.

CHAPTER ONE

Invisible Families

Why, you may ask, was this book named Invisible Families? The answer is two-fold.

First, there is an 'Invisible Family' to which many of our daughters and sons belong; this is their lesbian or gay 'family' — the people relied on for love and support. Even when their birth family is loving and understanding, this other family is needed. These friends share the same perspectives and understand the pressures of living in a predominantly heterosexual society. When the world in general discriminates against them, it is natural they will form their own 'family' — clubs, teams, venues, support groups and rights movements.

Second, because after talking with many people and reading the letters or questionnaires received from parents, other family members and from lesbian, gay or bisexual daughters and sons, I formed a strong impression that invisible is what we are. This was also borne out by our own experiences.

> We are 'invisible' because we are not well informed and tend to accept this situation.
>
> We are 'invisible' because while together we form a sizeable proportion of the population, many people do not want to know about us at all.
>
> We are 'invisible' because too often we allow some people's homophobia and/or religious bigotry to intimidate us and go unchallenged.
>
> We are 'invisible' because some of us, sometimes, dare not openly mourn our children and friends who have

died from AIDS or from suicide, due to relentless homophobic pressures.

We are 'invisible' because despite our common experience we feel alone.

Whether you are reading this in the first stages of numbed shock or because you have niggling doubts, want information, or are at war with yourself, or with your daughter, son, or others, the first point to remember is that while you may be 'invisible' you are not alone!

As parents we have a responsibility to bring up our children to be worthwhile citizens, with no formal training to help us do so. Consequently, when a daughter or son is seen to go against the mainstream of the moral, ethical, religious or legal standards to which we personally subscribe, we naturally become extremely anxious both for them and ourselves. For many reasons, when we discover our daughter or son is lesbian, gay or bisexual, we react according to the strongest messages we have ourselves been given about these standards and about homosexuality.

Easily overlooked or avoided is the fact that in choosing to bring children into this world we did not gain possession of them, and certainly they did not choose us! We do have a right to hope that blood ties, the love they have been given and the appreciation we have fostered between us will result in a two-way loving communication beneficial to us all as a family, but neither we nor they can demand it.

The time at which parents need to 'let go' and acknowledge a teenager's emergent adulthood is subject to debate and varies from individual to individual. Mainly it is decided by whether the teenager has been allowed to make mistakes, encouraged to try again, and given other opportunities to develop good judgment. Even so, strongly identified parents find it very hard to let go, particularly when there is an indefinable feeling or knowledge that something is not right and is troubling their child. Even if they are adults, we still worry about their well-being.

To discover sexuality issues are the cause of our daughter or son's problems may send shock waves of fear and panic through us. Many of us are right out of our depth, since sexuality may be for us a taboo subject, not discussed easily, in any sense. We are adrift with nothing to grasp to help us deal with the situation, except our basic love for our child.

Your immediate response might be: 'But I cannot condone homosexuality. It goes against my strongest natural (or learned, or religious, or rational) inclination and beliefs.' Or you might think: 'But I would not aid and abet them doing something equally wrong, like burglary.'

> If these are your responses, then the only possible reply is 'WHY?'
>
> Why is your thinking so?
>
> How exactly did you develop your beliefs and comparisons?
>
> Are you sure these are well informed?
>
> Can you, in fact, compare consensual sexuality to such acts as burglary?
>
> Are you saying your daughters or sons have a choice regarding sexual orientation?
>
> Are you right?
>
> Are you sure of this?

Answer yourself aloud. Go on replying and answering your reply with 'why?' until you are forced back to the beginning or to a position where you cannot honestly answer yourself with sure knowledge.

Only then, I believe, will you read this book from a clear, open, and non-prejudicial (un-pre-judged) position.

How can this non-judgmental position be achieved? I believe the answer is, by love, by true love for your daughter, son or family member. This is the love that is called 'unconditional', without any preconceived terms attached or laid down.

If you will start from a position of true love there is hope. If having read this book you cannot achieve full understanding or acceptance, that is your right.

Thinking constructively is hard work. It is much easier to believe what others tell us. I do not want you to believe me because I have written this book. My hope is that you will feel challenged to think about its contents and reach your own honest conclusions.

CHAPTER TWO

Being Told — Parents

In my early work on this book, I conducted an informal survey of parents, other family members, arid of lesbian, gay or bisexual sons and daughters. They were self-selected respondents, who contacted me as a result of interviews and articles which appeared in the media. They answered my questionnaire, and many wrote letters. The quotes which appear at the beginning of this and the following chapters are from these people.

I have included as many quotes as possible in the text of the book as it is important to acknowledge people's feelings. Often only the extremes are illustrated in books, rather than the ordinary experiences of everyday life. Each person's position is valid, each contributes to and builds the whole picture. A description of the survey itself is given in the appendix.

In this chapter, the quotes were in answer to the question, 'What were your first reactions when told?' What appears here is a selection from the responses received, which represent the main reactions.

About Gay Sons

'When my son told me he was gay it was a shock which didn't sink in for nearly two hours. Then I felt confused and started crying. There was sadness for him that his life would be much more difficult. There was also disappointment. I cried for three days. It was extremely difficult and I didn't stop until he said in desperation "Mum I haven't changed, I'm still me!" That pulled me up short — he was still my loving son. Since twelve years old he had been disturbed and upset by his feelings and retreated from his peer group and life in general. It was so sad.' (Mother)

'Initially I felt fear, shame, anger, confusion, guilt, disgust and pity for him. I was devastated. Now, seven years later, I still feel he didn't deserve this. My minister said he didn't know of anyone being "delivered". It's a cruel trick of nature. His father said he had always known it. My son says he is happy.' (Mother)

'I felt a rush of love for my son, mixed with sorrow and relief. At last there was an explanation for his difficult adolescence and the hurts. He went to Australia and was later saved from suicide by friends. He did not know his true sexuality until then, but I believe it was the reason for his being "at odds" with the world and his love/hate relationship with us. Now he has AIDS — it's heartbreaking.' (Mother)

'I hated knowing, while it wasn't said I could ignore it. Yet it was a relief. His father did his "nana" completely. He resented knowing even more than I did. To begin with we had hoped it would go away. Eventually after a long time he persevered and brought his partner home to tea, slowly from there we all became friends.' (Mother)

'We felt fear for him, grief, depression and shock. His marriage of three years was over and he had an eleven month old baby, we grieved for them too. For years I felt lonely and isolated particularly at church. I was afraid he would be rejected and despised — it takes a strong person to survive in a hostile community. What it does to their self-esteem can only be imagined.' (Parents)

'I always wondered about his sexuality since he was a small boy. He was shy and sensitive. He denied it for many years. Now his personality has blossomed and he is much happier. He says the years of not understanding himself nearly drove him to suicide and he has needed counselling for other problems due to the years of repression. I am so thankful he didn't become a statistic! He has two paternal uncles who are gay. One year after he did I "came out" too — with my heterosexual daughter's love and support. I have also blossomed and become much happier. I am sure it has a genetic cause.' (Mother)

'Confusion and relief, we knew something was hurting him. While I like my son, I cannot accept homosexuality as a comfortable situation. However he has to live out life as he sees it and will enjoy our support. I am troubled that there are far too many unstable relationships, that there will be difficulties for him in commercial life. No grandchildren for us.' (Father)

'Sorry I'd made things harder for him. Sorry he won't have kids of his own and a conventional marriage. Obviously though what has suited me wouldn't suit him. I worry about AIDS — just glad we haven't lost him. He can't come home too often because of cost and distance — it's good when he does.' (Father)

'He was only fourteen years old when he told me. He was being victimised at school. Fortunately we obtained good counselling and he was able to attend a Gay Youth Group. Even so I shed lots of tears and wondered why. I would have sacrificed everything for it to be otherwise for him. Initially I felt so isolated.' (Parents)

About Bisexual Sons

'Relief to know what was troubling him. Anger at the man who was the cause. His wife knew he was homosexual and he never stopped his gay relationships. I cannot and will never condone it.' (Mother)

'He already had fully developed AIDS, a double shock. He, his wife and family needed support. We were devastated, with no time to come to terms with his bisexuality or illness.' (Parents)

'Anguish at my parental incompetence. Guilt — where did I go wrong? He does not accept himself, uses drugs and has attempted suicide. Sadly, now he has HIV.' (Mother)

'Confusion because he had women friends, but acceptance almost at once.' (Mother)

About Lesbian Daughters

'I felt confused as if it was my fault and was ashamed at the way she was acting. From the age of thirteen years she acted as a boy, dressed as a boy, called herself by a boy's name and pursued relationships with girls. We got into arguments with other parents about this, Later I kicked her out of the house and told her not to return. She is twenty one now and in a happy lesbian relationship which deep down I'm pleased about. I get to see her quite often.' (Mother)

'I was numb, very cold inside and confused. My first thoughts were "Why me, what have I done to deserve this?" My husband didn't want to know. His first words were "Don't tell anyone about this. I don't want to see her again." '(Mother)

'Confusion, difficult to think of her like that, but I thought she needed a mate and was old enough to make up her own mind.' (Father)

'Fear for her, how would other people react to her? Her father retreated into silence. I love my daughter for herself, it would be easier if she was heterosexual, but she is happy and that is my foremost concern.' (Mother)

'Revulsion, shock, shame and anger. My husband never spoke of it, never discussed it with anyone. I can now speak of it to friends.' (Mother)

'Initially with shame, confusion and shock. My husband still won't accept it. Acceptance comes with time. It took me several years, I coped but didn't accept until recently.' (Mother)

'Anger, confusion. Both my lesbian daughters are loving and caring towards us. We love them very much. It is a hurt they did not want to give us, they knew it would cause problems at our church (other siblings are not gay).' (Mother)

About Bisexual Daughters

'Shocked but not surprised. Upset about her adolescent children.' (Mother)

'Distress for the ostracism they would both attract. Confused as to whether she was truly "lesbian" or reacting to a stormy marriage. Felt sure it was a lesson for her to learn — a necessary experience.' (Mother)

'Amused, as I wasn't surprised. My main concern was for her overall happiness, If the person she shares her life and sexuality with suits her then I'm satisfied.' (Mother)

Parents' First Reactions

Many parents wrote long explanations as to how and why they had felt as they had when told of their child's homosexuality. Many had known that their daughter or son was upset, unhappy or distressed. They had sensed lies and deception, had received seemingly undeserved negative or unloving behaviour, were worried about perceived anti-social behaviours, and had asked for explanations which had not satisfied. Now they knew the cause for these, their responses varied.

Often a parent reported experiencing a special rush of love, compassion and caring, as they realised how difficult things had been for their child. Some parents tried to 'fix' the problem, by taking their daughter or son to a doctor, psychologist or minister. This is a natural reaction — a parent's job is seen to include 'curing' a child's perceived 'hurts'. Others had sought out a counsellor for themselves, to help them understand, and to give them informed advice. There were also parents who were already well informed, having no prejudice or background which prohibited complete understanding.

Mainly these parents accepted their daughter or son's own self diagnosis, reasoning that they had taken years to sort this out and were not going against society for 'fun' or 'rebellion'. Frequently they grieved at the years she/he had suffered, not daring to risk telling, recognising that her/his parents were often the one stable love factor left in their confused situation.

These parents were saddened by her/his distress when

she/he did tell, whether it was from not wanting to hurt the parents or from fear of rejection. They also admired the nervous courage this had taken, and wrote of feeling honoured, privileged and proud of their courageous and truthful daughters and sons, who were ready to 'come out' and not live a life of deception.

Of course, not all responses from parents were positive or supportive — if they were, there would be no need for this book! The major negative responses reported were fear, grief, confusion, shock or anger, and guilt. These are discussed individually below and some in greater depth in Chapters 9 to 12.

All negative responses are fed by or based on a pseudo-reality, a blend of homophobic and unconsciously assimilated misinformation and fear. This is often reinforced by dogmatic religious or ethical ideas, by the media or by vague perceptions of 'proper' conventional stereotypes.

Negative first reactions to being told are common to many families and can be overcome. A majority of the parents in the survey who had such reactions later developed some, if not total, understanding over a period of weeks or months.

Fear

With both daughters and sons, fear was mainly due to the possible risks of STDs, especially of HIV/AIDS; possible victimisation from the known intolerance of society, including the workplace; and concern that when older their child would be lonely or unable to enjoy or raise a family.

An additional fear parents expressed was the possibility that not everything had been told to them. Had there been sexual abuse or molestation in the past? Was seduction involved? Were they being promiscuous, cross-dressing, or doing other 'things' too dreadful to imagine?

These are all valid fears in the light of the misinformation which abounds in our society. These fears were often described by parents as 'terrible', 'intense' and 'dreadful'.

There were many legitimate fears. Parents frequently felt completely 'out of their depth'. And the questions running chaotically through their minds were seemingly endless:

> How could they cope or help the best? Why had this happened?
>
> Where could they find help? How could they even ask for help?
>
> How could they begin to accept their child's lovers/partners?
>
> What do homosexual people actually 'do' sexually?
>
> How would they tell the other parent, or family or grandparents? Should this be done? Or is it solely their child's business?
>
> What of friends and neighbours, the priest/minister and friends at church — would they understand?
>
> Had they as parents done something to cause this?
>
> Would daughters and sons blame them?
>
> Or not understand how it was for them as parents, and/or not give them time to cope?

Grief

This was mentioned particularly by those parents who had come to realise how their child had been unthinkingly raised in strict heterosexual conformity from infancy. There was grief for those daughters or sons who had suffered deep depression and/or had finally attempted or considered suicide — often unsuspected by parents who felt anguish at not having known. And there was grief for those young people who had developed compulsive or self-destructive behaviours involving food, alcohol, and/or prescription or street drugs.

Parents also grieved for those who had suffered long periods of alienation from their family and from their church or ethical upbringing. And they grieved for those whose unhappiness and resulting low self-esteem had sent them into detrimental or transient sexual experimentations. Devastatingly, there were sons who had come home, frequently from overseas, to say not only that they were gay, but that they were HIV positive or had developed AIDS.

Parents also grieved for themselves, for the thought that, in many cases, there would be no next generation. It is natural to want grandchildren and, for some, to want to know that the family name(s) will be carried on. Some parents felt strongly rejected (if fleetingly), not only for their own sexuality, but for their way of life, standards and beliefs.

Shock

Many parents described their feelings of 'mind-numbing, stomach-churning, heart-rending shock'. It lasted for days, weeks, even months. According to individual temperament they were angry, abusive, rejecting, disgusted, silent, nagging, prayerful or tearful, in a range of combinations.

Parents, like daughters and sons, are all to some extent 'victims of victims' (see Chapter 12— Self-esteem). This happens particularly when our own upbringing, albeit with the best of parental intentions, has been somewhat controlling, conditional or even abusive; the next generation tends to react in the same way. In such instances homosexuality may be seen as being out of parental control, and the ensuing parental insecurity means a degree of rejecting behaviour (mostly temporary) by the parent(s) may follow.

Confusion

This encompasses all the other reactions. In my survey parents endlessly worried about how to make sense of it all.

Where to start? Who to trust? How, how did 'this' get hold of our child, especially if they were not what we had imagined as stereotypical? (A 'Mr Humphries' or perhaps Julian Clary?)

My survey showed homosexuality could appear in any family, and in any number in a family. Some gay sons were artistic, sensitive, more delicate as children — but many were football-playing, academically bright, noisy all-rounders who showed no signs of being different. Many delicate-looking sons, or quiet ones, who were not gay were in the same family as the tougher more rowdy sons who were. Some parents raised several sons, only one of whom was gay.

One mother reported one gay son, one lesbian daughter and three heterosexual children. Other mothers told of lesbian or gay offspring who were the oldest, the youngest, or those who were 'in-between'. Some were 'only' children.

Not all lesbian daughters were 'tomboys' or refused to wear dresses; none was said to 'hate' men, although some had been traumatised by men. Others were seen as strong-minded young women who had 'no time' for the male-dominated society. Many were seen to be no different from other young girls as they grew up.

Often families found there were 'hidden' lesbians and gays in the extended family among the nieces, nephews, aunts, uncles, or cousins. Twins, where both were lesbian or gay, were known. In other cases only one twin was so. Of course, in many twins neither is lesbian or gay.

Nature or nurture? Nothing was clear-cut. Every theory

produced more confusion, or contradicted the last one! After all, isn't this daughter or son the same person today that he or she was yesterday? Mind-numbing confusion was rampant!

Imposed Guilt

The mothers who responded seemed more prone to feelings of guilt than the fathers who responded. Maybe they recognised it easier or articulated it better. Mothers in New Zealand as a group, especially those born before 1950, suffer greatly from the conditioning which produced guilt in relation to their children.

I relate to this wholeheartedly from personal experience. Mine was the last generation brought up to conform without protest. There were few means of escaping the restrictions imposed and the rigid standards expected.

Many of us missed out on the liberating influences of the late 1960s. Dr Spock greatly confused the new mothers of this era! Frequently girls were denied tertiary education because their parents could not afford it. Work was easy to obtain, but employment for girls was seen as a stop-gap before the 'true vocation' of marriage. Women's needs often became totally sublimated in the expected attainment of 'perfect' motherhood and homes. When faced with the reality of homosexuality such mothers tend to become anxious and panic, and by misinformed inference feel themselves to have 'failed' in their parenting.

I received many responses from parents which indicated deep feelings of guilt associated with the belief that somehow they had 'made' their son or daughter gay or lesbian. I believe that the pervasiveness of a wide range of imposed guilt underlying their feelings about homosexuality is not recognised by many parents, nor validated by therapists. Neither is it appreciated by many lesbian, gay or bisexual daughters and sons, as relating to themselves or to their parents.

Frequently it is only when the burden of this imposed guilt, or more often the weight of any overlying resultant anxious, perfectionist, or compulsive behaviours, becomes so crippling that a breakdown in mental health occurs (that is, the person's ability to cope or function well in daily life deserts them), that help is sought, and the possible underlying causes are (hopefully) examined.

Denial

An alternative scenario may occur where the unrecognised imposed guilts become translated into a form of denial of the life situation. This may produce in parents, or in daughters and sons, the more self-acceptable emotions of fear, anger, panic or depressive 'free floating' anxiety attacks.

Frequently the whole spectrum of responses can be hidden under the general label of 'depression'. This is not necessarily a clinical depression but rather a deep sadness and confusion. Regrettably, it should be noted that some medical help, community support or therapy for depression still tends to deal with the symptom rather than the cause. As a result, the person can become more angry, anxious or panic-stricken, as they try even harder to rationalise these feelings as their own fault for a whole range of 'reasons'. They may berate themselves for not being more able, more intelligent, more ready to count their blessings, for not being able to cope or get on with life — while the underlying falsely imposed guilt is naturally reinforced by such thinking and increases!

Very few parents with negative responses blamed their daughters or sons, by thinking that their sexual orientation was a 'chosen preference' which could either be denied or not acted upon. Only rarely was it seen as an act of rebellion or a deliberate wish to hurt, shame or anger them. I believe any such long-held responses may be part of a deeper 'denial'; a reaction to perceived loss of status; and/or a possible shifting of the parental 'guilt factor' on to their child.

In Conclusion

As has been seen, parental responses to 'being told' were varied. Many wrote long explanations as to how and why they had felt as they did. Just as Ron and I had done, many parents felt guilty about accepting the dictates of their own upbringing or conservatism without question. Some blindly held on to what was familiar in this time of distress — not realising their reactions were possibly caused more by their own beliefs than by the sexuality of their daughters or sons. They felt they were somehow 'bad' parents. At this point it is important to recognise that by being unknowingly not well informed, many of us were unable to think or to feel otherwise.

Such parents believed that they had 'formed' their child. Cultural, psychiatric, psychological, criminological and religious 'common knowledge' or half-truths from earlier learning tumbled through their minds. Where had they gone wrong? The more they loved, feared and sorrowed, and the lower their own self-esteem, the worse they felt.

Other parents, particularly fathers, projected their own unacceptable feelings, including those of unrecognised denial or 'imposed guilt', on to their daughters, sons, wives or partners. They punished these people (and themselves) with angry silence, by refusal to discuss matters or to participate in family occasions. Some forced a 'choose me or them' situation. One grieving mother who insisted on nursing her son with AIDS was presented with a divorce as the required alternative if she did so — she chose the divorce!

Although the main responses from parents were basically the same for both sons and daughters, it seemed that mothers found it easier to accept their sons, perhaps because they were not as threatened as fathers were by their sons' being gay. Even if her sexuality was seen as being rejected, the mother's place in her son's life was still secure. In general, it seemed that a daughter's lesbianism was harder for parents to accept than a son's gayness; they felt confused, hurt or angry. A few reported feeling closer to her.

Conversely, with daughters, bisexuality seemed easier to accept than it was with sons. Some parents denied that it had happened or viewed it as a 'phase'. This enabled them to hold hope that their daughter would 'settle down' or 'come to her senses' one day. Where grandchildren were involved, understanding was even more difficult to attain. Anger and fear for the grandchildren were harder to resolve.

A few parents had retreated into martyrdom. They stated their love and 'acceptance' of the person — but not of their sexuality.

> 'Acceptance' — but they could not 'face' lovers or partners.
>
> 'Acceptance' — but they bemoaned the 'lack' of grandchildren.
>
> 'Acceptance' — but they were 'hurt' because it went against their principles, the church, or rigid standards.

It is widely recognised that in blaming others or searching for causes, people are often trying to retain a need to believe in a fair and just world. And in doing so they may feel better because the other person is assumed to be 'bad' or to have done something to bring the perceived problem upon him or herself Then they feel absolved of any possible 'blame'.

When an event such as homosexuality occurs in the family, for many parents this is outside of their own experience. In needing to be 'good' parents, they feel vulnerable and powerless. Having in effect believed this only happens to others, and lacking good information, they (temporarily) cannot cope.

It is hard for daughters and sons, brought up in a less inhibited era, not to be overwhelmed by such first reactions from parents, as have been listed here. Before coming out to parents, most lesbians and gay men go through their own trauma, dreading the possible adverse reactions. They scare each other half to death by tales of parental negative reactions! Sadly, there is enough outright rejection by families to make this a real possibility.

Even so, the fact still remains that most parents who responded to the survey, after being given support, information and time, did rally, reaching an at least partial, and in the main strongly positive, position of support and understanding.

CHAPTER THREE

Being Told — Other Family Members

About Lesbian Sisters and Gay Brothers

'At that time (1977) I thought I had understood. Listening to a tutor speaking on gay rights in 1991, I truly saw what she'd gone through from society. I wished I could go back and be really supportive.' (Sister)

'Fearful for him and selfishly for myself. What would the reactions of others be?' (Sister)

'He's my older brother, he got drunk and told me, I was instantly accepting — but very naive about it all then.' (Brother)

'Honoured to be told, then angry for him that he had to make a confession — I didn't have to announce my heterosexuality.' (Sister)

'I saw she had a sense of belonging she had never had before, was reassured and wished only her happiness.' (Sister)

'Concern — as I knew roughly how our parents would react, later cross as he wanted me to tell them!' (Sister)

'It was as though a piece in a jigsaw fell into place, I was glad she was freed to be a "whole" person, even though there would be difficulties for her.' (Sister)

'Sadness at the pain he endured over many years.' (Sister)

'Surprised enlightenment, anger, fear, discomfort.' (Female cousin)

'Confusion — he was married and had a child. Another older brother was gay (he died from AIDS), so I was fearful for him and for my parents who had been so hurt already.' (Brother)

'Relief — he had been withdrawn and troubled.' (Sister)

'I think his experiences as being gay have made me emotionally hard and extremely cynical — it's worrying.' (Brother)

"My brother didn't tell me, he took me to gay nightclubs unprepared, which made me feel uncomfortable and out of place.' (Sister)

The following responses are all from sisters.

'I know he'd love a permanent partner, I'm sad for him and worry about his health.'

'He may never have children, and would be good in the parenting role; it's sad.'

'It's OK while he's young, hope I won't have to become rejecting as he gets older — that he won't become a "dirty" old man.'

'HIV is a worry. Condoms are not "safe" only "safer" — they bust.'

'Partner changing too often? No stability in his relationships, or in the gay community?'

'Other people — who judge only by sexuality and not by the person. I worry about their rights in society.'

'Concerned that she had negative feelings and attitudes towards men, this has balanced out now, she is more tolerant and accepting towards them.'

This was not a large group amongst those in the survey and the majority responded with love and understanding. Even so, there was confusion and pain for some, and many siblings showed that initially they had not had adequate information or support for themselves.

When a sibling first learns that a sister is lesbian or a brother is gay, as with parents, negative feelings and prejudices may surface. This can be a shock if they have felt themselves to be open and honest people with a kindly attitude to others in general. They may worry greatly about such things as 'genetic inheritance' coming out in themselves — will they become homosexual later? They may worry about the stigma from society, and be afraid not only for their sister or brother but for themselves.

Many worried deeply for their brothers, sisters and parents. This is a heavy burden and responsibility. Like parents, siblings experience grief and fear and may suffer from adverse peer responses. I believe this has not been fully recognised. Siblings require better availability of support with counselling and certainly more information.

If you are a sibling reading this, or are a child of a lesbian mother or of a gay father, who is confused or worried, then I urge you to approach a lesbian or gay counsellor working for a well-established group, if you require more information and support than this book supplies. Good information will allow you to love your sister, brother or parent in a new and better way than before, and they will love and respect you for your support, which they need. Good information will help you all.

Parents' View of Brother/Sister Reactions

Parents were also asked how they saw the sibling response to a sister being lesbian, a brother being gay, or of either being bisexual. They reported:

- Brothers tended to be accepting, although several ignored the situation, and a few felt threatened and were hostile. Some younger ones felt pushed to prove their own 'macho' status — and were a worry.

- Sisters were more accepting but a few, mainly teenagers, were embarrassed. A few did not want to know, or had felt disgusted.

In any sibling relationships, parents need to accept that blood ties do not necessarily make for love or liking. Children are produced from a wide spectrum of parental genetic mix and each is unique. It can be wise to settle for the good manners due towards anyone.

Often, parental tension will affect the other relationships in the family. Once that is relieved, sibling relationships may improve.

Parents on the Response of Other Family Members

What other members of the family will think, and whether or not they should be told, are questions which trouble many parents. Interestingly, those who responded in the survey reported mainly positive reactions:

- Three stepfathers were positive and accepting. Many aunts and uncles said, 'We thought so, didn't you know?'

- Not all families told aged grandparents; the explanations were seen as too difficult for them to understand, or the necessary changes in values unlikely. However, some were very supportive and three grandmothers in their eighties shed a few tears, said 'So what', and loved their grandchildren as before. Two grandfathers of seventy-seven and eighty were reported as being loving and accepting.

As a general rule, family members should not be told without a daughter or son's permission. Although they may have told a parent or a friend, this is often only a first step in the 'coming out' process, which must proceed at the pace with which they are personally comfortable (see also Chapter 4).

CHAPTER FOUR

Telling Them – The Viewpoint of Daughters and Sons

Sons Telling Parents

'There was the whole gamut of negative human emotions. After six months positive reactions started creeping in. Now eighteen months later their views are on the whole very positive.'

'At first they were dumbfounded, then came a mixture of reactions — anger, denial, guilt — but most of all love. I wasn't thrown out on the street which I thought might happen. There were lots of questions as to "why" and fears about AIDS.'

'They were unaware of it. Mum burst into tears — she said because she thought I'd lead an unhappy life. She didn't personally know any gay men. My father came into the room, saw her crying, so I had to tell him too. He was totally unshocked and asked me if I wanted a drink!'

'Mother was shocked, had disbelief, denial, tears and pressured me to "change". Father was accepting — no real reaction — just said he wanted me to be happy.'

'Concern for me. They had very little understanding of what it means to be gay. I had to explain that we are not all sex mad and that most of us are well educated about AIDS.'

'Shock, tears, not wanting to be confronted with it, though they'd had some idea of it. Father said, "What have we done to deserve this; why tell us?"'

'Anger, shock, rejection. It precipitated my leaving home and a period of detachment from my parents (but not my siblings). Gradually relations improved and Mother is becoming very accepting.'

'My mother tended to blame herself and thought she was at fault somehow with my upbringing. She then refused to accept it and subscribed to my father's view that I was too young to know and it was "a phase".'

'Mother seemed totally accepting and relieved to know. Father was very angry and hurt by my disclosure.'

'Shock and concern, but support for me. Fear for themselves in that they didn't want others to know. Fear for me and my future.'

'My father was speechless — wanted not to talk — to change the topic. Mother was concerned for the negative implications I would face from others and in my work, but primarily was accepting of what I had said.'

'Shock, tears, questions of where did they go wrong. After a month of no contact I gave them a full explanation of my sexuality, how private it is, how because I loved and trusted them that I wanted to be honest and not live my life as a lie. Then they were accepting.'

'My parents are deceased. I recently told my brothers, who reacted with disbelief. They still do not believe it and try to introduce me to women.'

'A sudden switch-off. It's NOT happening. Will do anything but sit down and talk it out. Postponed any discussion until "later" — perhaps hoping it may go away?'

'My father is dead. My mother was very emotional (as was I) with tears. At first I think she was shocked but that gave way to guilt that she hadn't any idea of what I had been going through all these years, yet she clearly knew something was wrong. She was concerned for me — that as a gay man it may be harder for me especially in my profession.'

'Mother said: "Gay", "AIDS", "Death" — then fainted — all in thirty seconds. Father didn't say anything for one hour.'

'Telling my parents I am gay took a lot of courage, which is why I confided my sexuality to someone on the Gay Switchboard first. It took me four months of attending newcomer meetings before I could tell them.'

Daughters Telling Parents

'Father's reaction was, "So what". Mother's was, 'But I always dressed you in pretty frocks".'

'Acceptance, they told me they'd known for two years.'

'Anger, concern for what they felt they had lost, guilt, accusations at me, "What will everyone think?", rejection, and discomfort with me.'

'Very angry. Changed their wills. No contact for two years, then threatening letters and phone calls for about another two years.'

'Mother agreed it was harder to live a lie, but preferred I wasn't "obvious". Father wanted me to have a home and family. He accepts that I am happy, but is not comfortable with homosexuality. They both accept me and my partner for who we are and the joy that we bring each other.'

'I was very lucky they have both handled it quite well, saying if that's what makes me happy in life, then they are happy for me.'

'Mother said she could accept me, didn't understand why or how I was lesbian and disapproved of my lover. Father still accepted me as his daughter.'

'There must have been some shock but they are totally supportive of myself and my partner. They think it good to see me happy for the first time in many years. Dad thought I was "different" for quite some time before my coming out. My mum and dad are great.'

'Mum found out before she spoke to me and spent a week crying about it. When we did talk she asked me to see a priest, which I did to keep her happy. I think the label "lesbian" was hardest for her to accept and the idea of sex between women. She said my being lesbian made her feel embarrassed around her friends and as though she'd caused it somehow.'

'Shock, anger, concern plus "Maybe we should send you to a psychiatrist" from my father. "I would rather you were dead than be one of those" from my mother.'

'My mother said she had "suspected" I was a lesbian. She seemed concerned that I was making a decision that would affect the rest of my life in a bad way, but made it clear that she loved me even though I had made that decision.'

These sons and daughters were responding to Question 6 in my survey, 'What were your parents' first reactions when you told them you were lesbian, gay or bisexual?' For parents, the whole picture of a daughter or son's 'coming out' is hard to grasp or define. If we have ourselves come out on some of the issues involved, maybe we have gained a little understanding. But our daughters and sons are the only ones who really know how it is for them.

One woman, Jo Crowley (Isherwood Trust Newsletter Sept 1991), writes that although she's been 'out' for twenty years she still feels a residual anxiety associated with further coming out. She explains:

'Your sexuality alludes to a very personal part of your life and also it's actually no one else's business. But we are in the unusual position of having to prove our normalcy, so coming out is very important, as well as good for us.

'Over the years I have tried to analyse this fleeting feeling of anxiety, knowing full well that it can be crippling for many members of our community. Because we have knocked over so many homophobic hurdles since 1968, I feel this anxiety could be the key to our self oppression: the constraints we impose on ourselves.

'If I named it, I thought] would be able to recognise it in the future, and then make it impotent instead of paralysing. I called it "Rejection Anxiety".

'Coming Out is a never-ending process. If I am getting close

to someone then there will come the "moment of truth" at which point they will become aware that I am a lesbian. At this point I am at my most vulnerable. Either they will say "Sure, I knew all along' or "Yeh, me too", or they will reject me, awkwardly.

'However, we can survive awkwardness, we don't need to give "rejection anxiety" as much power as we do. Coming Out is actually a wonderful process that usually gets a very positive reaction, creates open friendships, is personally empowering — and it's very good for them (the person we are coming out to) as well ... [by doing so] we make huge little inroads into [our own and] social homophobia.'

Coming Out in Stages

In their replies to the questionnaires, many daughters and sons referred to the 'never-ending process' attached to coming out, which tends to follow stages of self-awareness. Beginning with self-recognition, the person coming out usually proceeds to other lesbian or gay friends or a straight friend, then to possibly a family member and/or parents. Eventually (a major step this one) they will come out to the workplace. Finally, when frustrated with the pretence and when they feel strong enough, they come out to everyone as appropriate. Some then move into activist or support groups.

Coming out is not automatic, neither do the stages always progress. It is possible to never acknowledge one's homosexual orientation, to live in constant stressed denial, or to remain at any stage of the process. Parents have been known to reinforce or insist on this denial, or demand a cover-up of orientation.

Coming out takes time. It is necessary to be gentle and kind to oneself and others. One gay man, who works for a gay support group, estimates the whole process may take several years, from self-awareness to living openly with a lover or partner. There can be strong and valid reasons for not coming out. But at least partial coming out is to be encouraged, as it is vital to mental health and is a strengthening process towards a balanced self-understanding. Today's young people are becoming self-aware earlier, so parents have a greater than ever obligation to supply guidance, support and resources for such daughters and sons.

I asked Felix Donnelly, Director of the Youth Link Trust in Auckland, if, from his experience in counselling, he felt that being self-aware earlier made coming out easier for young people. He said, 'No, I don't find it so. Indeed it can make it harder. The school environment is often hostile. It can lengthen the period of stress before they can meet others like themselves or find support. Neither is it evidenced in any change in the suicide figures.'

In times of high unemployment, economic depression, and family stress, the mental health of all young people is at risk. For a young lesbian or gay brought up with strong heterosexual expectations, the personally frightening sexual confusion they may experience serves to heighten the general problems faced by all teenagers.

Counsellors I spoke with agreed that advice and guidance is necessary, to combat the negative self-images which may be gathered and internalised during childhood and adolescence. Parents need to be aware that the stresses their lesbian, gay or bisexual young people generally encounter in growing up can and often do result in some form of substance abuse (see Chapter 9).

Other Issues

Responses to the questionnaires raised other issues, and the following comments relate to these.

Several daughters and sons had sensed an emotional difference from early childhood, and/or a feeling of not fitting into peer groups or meeting family expectations. This was frequently not recognised as being due to homosexuality until puberty and later.

On realising their homosexuality, their own first reactions had been mainly shock and denial. Many tried valiantly not to be 'different'. Most sons were in their later teenage years, early twenties or older, before they dared to 'come out' or to physically express their orientation. Daughters tended to be older still in coming out. Some who had not previously known what had been 'wrong', reported relief.

They said parents need to be aware that today, with better information available, young people are coming out earlier, even at puberty, and that they need much love, understanding, acceptance and guidance.

For daughters and sons, the strict assumptions of compulsory heterosexuality they had been brought up with had led in many instances to a complete submersion of orientation. For some, marriage had brought disillusionment and a rough awakening, often with a further sense of failure. Many unhappy years of denial and/or guilt were then experienced (see Chapter 5).

Negative parental reactions were reported as 'devastating' by daughters and sons. The most common reaction seen was disbelief and denial of the fact, with such expressions as 'Go and see a priest, psychiatrist, or counsellor', 'Are you sure?', 'Don't mention it again', or an attitude of 'If we ignore it, it might go away'.

Other reactions they reported included guilt, anger, shock, disgust, grief, shame, surprise and concern for their daughter/son's health, and/or for them/themselves socially, and fear of the possible adverse reactions from other family members, society, and the workplace.

Daughters and sons felt strongly that as of right they were entitled to love and support, backed by a willingness to rethink the issues, from parents. When this was not received it hurt deeply. In the main, where daughters and sons persevered or were prepared to give information and support, their efforts eventually resulted in happier understanding and acceptance.

There was great sadness at the non-acceptance by parents and other family of lovers or partners, even after years of a committed relationship: the missing invitations to family occasions, the ignoring of birthdays and anniversaries, and the 'blaming' of partners as being the 'cause' of their adult child's sexual orientation.

Often daughters' and sons' own perceptions of why they were lesbian or gay initially mirrored their parents' beliefs, particularly where imposed guilt and misinformation had been assimilated. In general, the same explanations for this are applicable. A few could not be self-accepting and were utterly confused and unhappy. Others knew it was 'right' for themselves but still wondered 'why' it had happened.

What determines sexual orientation and what parents thought might be influencing factors are discussed in Chapter 6.

CHAPTER FIVE

What About Marriage? Gay or Lesbian Spouses/ Parents

About Gay Partners/Parents

> 'I had great fear for him (because of AIDS); was sorry for him, if he'd known as a teenager, his life would have been different. Now he has children and may not have if he'd known. But would his life have been happier if he'd known? The older children understand. I would always look after him if he was sick.' (Wife)

This couple are still married. He says recognising and doing something about his being gay has been a most difficult experience; there has been both gain and loss. He loves his family and has no intention of not honouring his obligations. Now in a committed gay relationship, he divides his time between both homes.

> 'His homosexuality has been a long miserable on-again off-again problem as he tried to deny this over twenty years. He really tried not to be. He said to my daughter, "I love your mum, I will always love her." We are now separated. It was very hard to adjust and I miss him. It worries me that his "friend" is younger than his own son.' (Wife)

> 'I was shocked and confused, especially concerned for my mum although she was understanding. It didn't make any difference to my relationship with him. He's had a gay relationship now for a couple of years. I don't see him much. I worry about AIDS.' (Daughter)

'I had suspicions for a while before he told me. My sisters don't mind. My mother was angry that he'd married her. I've lived with him for four years and know his friends who are nice to me. I don't feel threatened. I'm straight.' (Son)

A phenomenon of recent times has been the numbers of people in their thirties and forties and older, often married, who felt able, given changing social attitudes, to stop struggling against their homosexuality arid act on it. Often the experience has been painful to themselves and family members, particularly their partners.

I had first-hand experience of this when a gay man, pushed by convention into marriage, explained how he had waited for his children to grow up before parting from his wife of over twenty years. He was holding hands with his new male partner, and with tears in his eyes said it was the first time he had been truly in love. His family had totally rejected him.

Several older lesbians and gay men related with sorrow and anger their feeling that they had in effect been duped into marriage; they are only now courageously coming out after years of dissatisfaction and unhappiness. Many are genuinely fond of their spouses and love their children, but are desperate to be 'whole' and stop living a lie. Some have been churning over finally taking such action since the Homosexual Law Reform Act, with great mental strain and suffering. It is not easy to break up a marriage of many years. Again, it is scary to risk 'going it alone' in life and face rejection, particularly when most needing support. Others, however, reported receiving loving support.

Many of the men had been totally dismayed at the effect sex with their wives produced. It was not fulfilling for them or for their wives, although contrary to yet another myth many gay men are capable of heterosexual intercourse and of fathering children. Further, they told of other gay and/or bisexual men who remained closeted, yet sought transient sexual liaisons with male partners in situations fraught with danger of discovery. Such men are likely to have low self-esteem. They may be at particular risk from the abuse of drugs and/or alcohol, from HIV/AIDS or suicide.

Older lesbians in particular often had not recognised that they were not heterosexual. The conditioning they received to be ultra feminine from early childhood, or after they were considered too old to be 'tom boys', was later reinforced by peer pressure. Frequently they had gone into marriage as virgins, desperately hoping it would be 'all right on the night'. It was a sad awakening. They too had been at risk from the abuse of drugs and/or alcohol, the problems of anorexia, bulimia, or suicide.

For a loving partner to be faced with a husband or wife's bisexuality or homosexuality can be an enormous shock, as well as utterly confusing, even if the partner has been aware for some time of the conflict their husband or wife was experiencing. There may be understandable anger at their 'betrayal' and, on the part of the wife, fears that she might have been put at risk of HIV/AIDS or other STDs. It can take time, counselling, and courage to overcome such concerns, and to deal with the surrounding issues.

For some of those who responded to the survey, their reactions involved fear, loss of self-respect, anger, conflict, and/or blaming, which frequently became destructive to all involved, including any children. Often these responses were based on the preconceptions and misinformed beliefs we observed when discussing parents and which can cause panic. When other family members 'took sides', it was often more unhelpful than supportive.

On the other hand, where the husband or wife (and the lesbian, gay or bisexual partner) were able to project understanding and love, this greatly eased the trauma for everyone. Their forbearance was respected and it enabled present and future decisions to be made with a sense of care, which helped all involved.

It is important to acknowledge and gain some understanding about the deeply traumatic issues where latent homosexuality or bisexuality is experienced. The reasons behind these are discussed further in Chapters 6 to 8, 10 and 11.

No questionnaire responses were received from children of lesbian mothers. As with siblings, this whole area is under-researched and such families, by inference, are not well supported. It would arguably be difficult for many such children to understand or accept a parent's change from perceived heterosexuality.

CHAPTER SIX

So, What Determines Sexual Orientation?

'A person with homosexual status is one who has the potential to fall in love only with someone who has the same body sex-the same genital and body morphology - as the self For a heterosexual, the morphology must be that of a person of the other sex. For the bisexual it may be either.

'A sexual status (or orientation) is not the same as a sexual act. It is possible to participate in homosexual acts and even be cajoled or coerced into participation, without becoming predestined to have a permanently homosexual status — and vice versa for heterosexuality ...'
Dr John Money, *Gay, Straight and Inbetween* (1990)

This chapter has the silent sub-title, 'And Does This Matter?' It provides information and challenges some of the myths that surround homosexuality. In general, parents are so conditioned to the assumption that being heterosexual is the right and desirable norm, that to put this perspective aside and consider other points of view is for many extremely difficult. This conditioning is fostered by those who are obsessed with 'curing' or preventing homosexuality.

So what did parents think had caused their daughter or son to be homosexual or bisexual? When parents were asked to consider this question many showed by their answers the conditioning and misinformed 'common knowledge' they had absorbed. The following quotes are taken from the parents' strongly affirmative answers to Question 15 of the questionnaire, which asked:

'Did you feel guilty? Think that as a parent you had brought them up wrongly? Been the "cause"?

'If "Yes" can you explain why this is so?' Over half the respondents said 'yes' or 'partly' to this question — all but one were mothers.

On Gay or Bisexual Sons

'I gave him birth, now he might suffer.'

'Examined every negative thing I'd done to him.'

'Felt home and upbringing must have caused it.'

'Knew overprotective mothers were the fault, thought I must have been one, but wasn't sure.'

'Had been very close to my sons, but only one was gay.'

'His father was quiet, yet loved him dearly — had he been too passive?'

'His father is violent and frightened him.'

'Vague knowledge of Freud's teachings. Society's attitudes.'

'I was very stressed when I was pregnant with him, had it caused some developmental hiccup?'

'We sent him to a single-sex boarding school.'

'I encouraged his sensitivity and didn't make him play sports —perhaps I should have.'

'I'd been taking the contraceptive pill until right before he was conceived and he was premature.'

'He was an intelligent, difficult, uncooperative child; had we been too hard on him?'

'He was so sensitive, artistic and bright; had we been too soft with him?'

'I positively wanted a daughter, did my thinking affect my baby — it must have been my fault.'

'I was a sole mother and he had only sisters — did the upbringing in an all-feminine home affect him?'

'My marriage broke up when he was seven; he lived with a dominant grandmother.'

'His father died when my son was young, he clung to me.'

'I nearly miscarried at four months; had it affected him?'

'Parents are responsible for how a child turns out; our fault.'

'He said it was our fault as we argued a lot' [And other variations of blame from a few sons].

'He was small and "sassy"; picked on all through school.'

'He was big and gentle; teased at school as a poof.'

'As a young child he had only girls to play with.'

On Lesbian or Bisexual Daughters

'Gone wrong in my parenting somehow, my fault.'

'Could I have done things differently?'

'Had I been a domineering mother?'

'She suffered abuse in the family.'

'Stressful early life, lots of moves, little money, I was depressed, not enough quality support in her teens.'

She's adopted — early trauma.'

'Thought it must be my side of the family, but found my in-laws have two of the same.'

'She had a broken home, very violent father, then objected strongly to any male friends I made.'

'Her father made her anti-men.'

'I must have given her the wrong amount of chromosomes.'

'Her name could be a boy's name too.'

If all these 'causes' for guilt (and for homosexuality) were right, every daughter and son ever born who experienced such circumstances would surely be homosexual — which obviously they are not! It puts into perspective the terrible mixture of guilt, fear and panic parents felt.

These completely serious and honest beliefs and ideas plagued parents during those early weeks and months of knowing. For many, it was four or five years and more before better information gave understanding and relief from the worry of guilt.

These false ideas are rife throughout society. If you identify with any of these, be assured that you are NOT alone in this!

In this chapter we look at some of the most common misconceptions. In following chapters we explore how these fears, half-truths and poor information have been assimilated and accepted.

Conversion

One common fear centres around 'learned behaviour' or 'conversion'. The New South Wales Anti-Discrimination Board Report 1982 found fears that lesbians and gay men, such as teachers, would 'convert others or promote their lifestyle' were unfounded.

Many parents and others express concern that teenagers may go through a developmental phase in which intense friendships develop with another person of the same gender — while perhaps not knowing this is a relatively common experience and does not necessarily mean they are homosexually pre-disposed.

These 'conversion or seduction' theories imply homosexuality is an opinion, belief or creed to which people can be converted. In effect, it judgementally says homosexuality is an undesirable 'alternative lifestyle'.

I believe that with good information teenagers are well able to differentiate such feelings. None of my correspondents or the homosexual young people I spoke to stated such a situation as being a possible 'cause' for their homosexuality. They did not want to be 'different', for to be the same as, and accepted by, their peers is for most a vital need. Many had been victimised, so the need to be accepted added to any problems associated with overcoming homophobia and making a happy, positive affirmation of their sexuality.

I questioned Stephen Jacobs, a respected counsellor in Auckland, on this. In his opinion and experience it was clear that if any persons who had been abused as children or young teenagers and thought this was the origin of their homosexuality, then they had not dealt with the confusion such trauma caused and should seek help from well-informed counsellors. This opinion was affirmed by several mature gay men, who counsel others.

It is now recognised that peer group homosexual experience is not inductive to any permanent homosexual behaviour in those heterosexually orientated, although research on this is sparse.

Psychological Theories

Science is supposedly by definition 'objective', but in reality scientists still make 'value judgements' according to both their personal beliefs and the prevailing attitudes of the times. In medicine, homosexuality has variously been seen as degenerate, a constitutional abnormality, a biological anomaly, mental illness or a personality disorder.

However, recent psychiatric and psychological approaches define homosexuality as a variant of sexuality and not as a mental illness. Homosexuality was removed from the Australian and New Zealand College of Psychiatrists' list of mental illnesses in 1972. The American Psychiatric Association resolved in 1973 — after decades of defining homosexuality as an illness — to delete homosexuality from the list of personality disorders in the association's Diagnostic and Statistical Manual. This action revised earlier Freudian and post-

Freudian psychoanalytical theory on homosexuality. Freud's view had been that homosexuality was caused by possessive, dominant mothers and weak or absent fathers. In his famous letter to the American mother of a homosexual son he reassured her: '... it cannot be classified as an illness; we consider it to be a variation of sexual function, produced by a certain arrest of sexual development.'

Unfortunately the damage done by those who took up his theories and extended them was far-reaching. Attempting to find or effect a 'cure', rather than to understand the condition, and psychoanalytically influenced, the post-Freudians did much harm.

One of the most harmful works from this point of view was *Homosexuality: A Psychoanalytic Study* by Irving Bieber et al (1962). The study had been made by gathering information not from homosexuals, but from psychiatrists who filled in questionnaires on case histories of clients. These would only have included homosexuals who were unhappy in the generally repressive climate of the times and/or disturbed enough to seek therapy.

Bieber claimed to have found certain personality traits which were 'typical' of homosexual men, such as excessive need for sexual gratification, narcissism, voyeurism, and/or exhibitionism. These 'traits' were seized on by the public, by bigots and by the media, and gave rise to further myths, homophobia and discrimination.

Bieber's theory was that in the 'homosexually-inductive' family, the parents' fear of masculine assertiveness caused them to curb such behaviour, leading boys to show a preference for feminine behaviour and activities.

Cornelia B. Wilbur, one of Bieber's co-workers, applied similar ideas to lesbians and their parents. She found the 'typical' mother of a lesbian daughter to be controlling, the 'typical' father to be kind but unassertive. Variations on the themes of these and other post-Freudians have today filtered through to a brew of 'common knowledge' (see Chapter 10).

In the 1970s the 'helping professions' turned away from the idea that homosexuality was a personality disorder, but publicly the damage was done. It is no wonder that some parents — who were reaching adulthood or newly married at this time — later fell back on half-remembered misinformation when told of their daughter's lesbianism or son's gayness!

Examples from my survey showed some people had perceptions of gay men as being effeminate, promiscuous, emotionally hysterical, sexually uncontrolled, or as seducers of small boys. These are unfounded. It is notable that rape, paedophilia and incest are predominantly committed by heterosexual men. However, male heterosexuality is not usually defined or discussed with this in mind. Similarly, many people had assumed all lesbians were masculine, 'butch', aggressive women who hated men.

Knowing no better, caring parents who found some evidence that they had been 'typical' in the raising of a child who is lesbian or gay immediately tended to worry deeply, believing they were the 'cause'. Besides, people they knew and respected told them this was how it must be. However, any such evidence of 'typicality' is a coincidence, not a 'cause'. If every child who had a disadvantaged childhood was thereby 'made' lesbian or gay, the numbers of heterosexual people would be dramatically reduced. (Interestingly no one accuses parents of 'causing' heterosexual children!)

Biological Theories

The early psychoanalytical approach did not satisfactorily explain the cause of homosexual orientation, because no childhood experiences are identical and no two individuals are ever exactly alike. Also, why did other children brought up by the same parents have a differing sexual orientation as adults?

The search for a biological cause starts with an assumption that sexual desire is primarily, if not exclusively, determined by biological factors designed for regeneration. This assumption may be questioned on the grounds that humans are infrequently motivated to sexual activity by a desire to reproduce. Indeed, heterosexual behaviour often involves active avoidance of conception.

Biologists turned to the study of chromosomes and hormones in the 1940s and 1950s, but at first found little relationship with sexual orientation. However, Dr Michael Bailey reported recently from Northwestern University in Evanston, Chicago, USA:

> *'We found that 52% of the identical twin brothers of gay men were also gay, compared with 22% of fraternal twins, compared with 11 % of genetically unrelated (adoptive) brothers; which is exactly the kind of pattern you would want to see if something genetic were going on.'*
> (*NZ Herald* 16/12/91)[1]

In 1991 a new study, from comparisons made in autopsies of brains from homosexual men who had died from AIDS, and heterosexual men, some of whom had died from AIDS and some who had not, has suggested there is a structural difference in the brain between homosexual and heterosexual men. It was not a large study and did not make a full comparison with the brains of women, but fits with the twin studies and theories that sexual orientation could be determined by factors related to certain hormones affecting prenatal development.[2]

Since this book was written scientists at the United States National Institutes of Health have reported in Science magazine that Dr Dean Hamer et al have discovered five genetic

---

1 A fuller report on this can be found in the *Washington Blade* 20/12/9 1, Vol.22, No.51.

2 Report by Dr. S. LeVay, Salk Institute for Biological Studies, San Diego, USA, in Science Vol. 253 August 1991.

markers in a region on the X chromosome known as Xq28 sitting on a stretch of DNA consisting of several hundred genes which analysts say suggest a homosexual gene or genes (*NZ Herald*, 17th July 1993, Reuter, Washington).

On 31st October 1995, while being interviewed on Radio NZ by Kim Hill, Dr Hamer reported other family genetic/chromosomal findings extending and supporting this earlier research.

None of these studies are as yet conclusive, requiring further work and development but they will please those people eager to establish a biological base for sexuality. Certainly there are strong indicators suggesting biological involvement, although it is not precisely known how genetics and/or hormonal development, either prenatally and/ or postnatally, may be combined or linked to affect sexual orientation and/ or sexual behaviour.

Conclusion

Theories of seduction or conversion have been discredited, as have the psychoanalytical theories of the post-Freudians. Disagreement remains as to whether sexual orientation is determined by environmental[3] or biological factors or some combination of these. As the New Zealand AIDS Foundation says: 'There is considerable agreement that sexual orientation as such is fixed by the age of three or four at the latest. In other words, sexual orientation must be considered an "intractable" human characteristic.'

At the beginning of this chapter I quoted John Money on homosexuality. He further explains in *Gay, Straight and Inbetween:*

'A heterosexual man or woman does not become heterosex-

3 'Environmental' does not relate solely to parental influence - a belief which is common. Rather it implies the whole influence from society to be heterosexual from infancy.

ual by preference. There is no option, no plan. Becoming heterosexual is something that happens — an example of the way things are, like being tall or short, left-handed or right-handed, colour blind, or colour seeing. Being homosexual is no more a preference than being heterosexual ... One either is; or is not bisexual, homosexual or heterosexual.'

The genetic gender of a human embryo is determined by several factors. As Lewis Wolpert, Professor of Biology as Applied to Medicine at University College, London, writes in his book *The Triumph of the Embryo*, Oxford University Press (1991):

'After six weeks of (embryonic) development ... the primary sex (ie. gender; male or female) has already been determined, and now the secondary characters come under hormonal control...

'(All) embryos are basically females unless exposed to male hormone.'

Research is still needed as to how hormones may affect sexual orientation, the brain and sexual behaviour. Just what does govern the quality and quantity of these hormones and exert changes not only in-utero and at puberty, but also at other times during life's developmental processes?

Like many other parents, Ron and myself would have preferred there to be a clear-cut biological 'cause' explaining homosexual orientation. Challenging the assumptions surrounding compulsory heterosexuality is stressful and difficult — frequently our generation was raised with no conception of other sexualities. And if heterosexuality was right for us, we had no personal need to seriously challenge our beliefs.

Having listened to many others involved in these issues and from our own experiences, we feel sure that the basic cause of homosexuality will one day prove to be genetically governed and chemically predisposed. As parents we produce a wide range of genetic possibilities in a child. Genes determine inheritance of physique, hair structure, eye colour, temperament, brain power, musical talent, and much, much more.

Some people fear that should genetics or hormones be confirmed, either partly or wholly, as a determinant of differing sexual orientations, that in future scientific engineering might be practised to eliminate homosexuality or those so orientated. I find this untenable. It would foster a Nazi-type concept of a 'master race', and the validity of naturally created different sexualities would be judgementally denied.

Furthermore, it is known that factors both physiological and/or psychological can intermingle in many complex ways and alter brain chemical patterns. Science does not as yet know exactly how all these interact.

As parents, we carry tendencies to behaviour and learned responses which began for us many generations ago and which are based on inherited imprints. These responses are, Ron and I believe, also largely biologically/chemically predetermined. Just as there is physical DNA, we feel, there will one day be found a similar emotional or psychological equivalent. Geneticists are rapidly becoming aware of many previously unknown predispositional conditions, and we could now perceive that homosexual orientation to be but another complex variant of humanity.

I also spoke with someone who challenged me with the thought that it is arguably more pertinent to be worried about what 'causes' heterosexuality in these times of alarming over-population of the planet. Indeed, does human society still wish for an uncontrolled reproductive sexuality as encouraged (or supported by uninformed default) by many state, church or medical factions? This may well be a concept which society worldwide will need to deal with in the near future.

CHAPTER SEVEN

Sexual Behaviour — A Continuum

When Alfred Kinsey reported the results of his research in *Sexual Behaviour in the Human Male* (1948) and *Sexual Behaviour in the Human Female* (1953), there was a shocked response from around the world. Kinsey had devised a scale to measure sexual interest and behaviour patterns and, as Dr Max Abbott in Homosexuality: An Overview of Research and Professional Opinion (1985) describes,

> *'Kinsey's study made it clear that it is not possible to maintain a sharp distinction between heterosexuals and homosexuals ... (for) while people do tend to cluster towards one or other of the two ends of the Kinsey scale, there is an overlap.'*

And he added, 'While other scales have since been developed and other surveys conducted, Kinsey's study from the late 1940s remains, in some ways, the most adequate.'

Largely through Kinsey's research, a ten per cent figure for the incidence of homosexual behaviour in the Western population has come to be generally accepted, but is this right? Although there have been many studies in different countries, the methodology for collecting data has varied.

In 'Is 10% Too High?', a *Frontiers* news magazine article (27 September 1991), Bill Geiger quotes Tom Smith, director of the General Social Surveys at the American National Opinion Research Center, as saying,

> *'[Homosexuality] is one of the most difficult things to measure. It's personal and intimate, some people won't admit to*

> *it ... Many people won't give a true response which leads to under-reporting.'*

Geiger also quotes Charles Turner, programme director for the Center in Research Studies and Statistics at the Research Triangle Institute in Washington DC,

> *'Nobody really knows what the right number is. The 10 per cent figure is purely speculative. It's clear that current studies have been negatively biased, but we don't know by how much. This field has been starved — there is no great body of research data. This has hurt in helping to understand the AIDS epidemic.'*

Geiger says many anti-gay politicians have seized upon the lowest of the lower-bound estimates, developed their own figures using flawed methodology, and rounded down figures ... in an effort to significantly reduce the estimated gay population.

Turner further comments, 'Anyone who uses lower-bound figures is missing the point. Since we can't precisely estimate the homosexual population, [using lower-bound estimates in an] attack runs contrary to everything we know.'

Geiger concludes, 'So despite its flaws, Kinsey's estimates remain the benchmark by which most authorities reference.'

It is not always easy from brief reports to know whether studies give percentages for exclusive orientation only or refer to a behaviour continuum. Some include lesbians, and others do not.[1] It is most necessary when quoting statistics to ascertain the criteria which applied to that particular research, and also consider how it was funded, by whom it was commissioned, and for what purpose.

However, let us not forget that the claims of gay men and lesbians to a fair deal in our society are based on their hu-

1 Geiger gives a list of some recent studies and percentages for those wanting to research this further.

manity and citizenship, and not on their making up a certain proportion of a population. If only one per cent of the population is exclusively homosexual, this can only provide a lower-bound estimate, and in any case does not justify discrimination.

No matter what the actual percentage, as a parent I find it interesting to speculate that if every lesbian or gay man has only two other people closely concerned for their welfare, this must amount to a significant proportion of the population who have a keen personal interest in the issues relating to homosexuality.

What Homosexuals 'Do'

When the questionnaire responses were collated, it was apparent that lesbian, gay, or bisexual behavioural sexual practice is one of the most difficult areas for many parents to acknowledge or understand. Half of the daughters and a third of the sons indicated that their sexuality was not (or only partially) accepted, while most had felt accepted as people. This is obviously a contradiction in terms, for sexuality is not divisible from the person.

Furthermore, that such sons and daughters are uncritically accepting this division between their orientated sexuality and their whole selves is very detrimental, for it arises from an unperceived erosion of their self-esteem forged over many years by the pressures to conform with society's false norms regarding 'desirable' heterosexuality

For parents, the non-acceptance of homosexuality is frequently caused by the emotional responses to presumed sexual practice. These presumptions need to be firmly laid aside, so that lesbianism, homosexuality or bisexuality may be considered without prejudice.

As parents Ron and I found it helpful to acknowledge that we do not usually view the heterosexual people we meet solely on the basis of their perceived sexuality or presumed sexual behaviour. Most people accept others for their personality or skills — surely this should apply equally to our daughters, sons and their partners.

Secondly, parents will find it helpful to think back to their own experiences of being in love and attracted to their partner. Think about how deeply this was felt: how sexuality was but a part of the wider and whole loving commitment; how hurt we would have been if our choice was rejected by our family.

There are considerable differences between men and women in how they experience sexuality, whether heterosexual or homosexual. However there is less difference between lesbian, gay, bisexual, or heterosexual sexual practice than many people realise:

- Anal penetrative sex is not exclusive to gay or bisexual men. It is known to be regularly practised by heterosexual couples. It is also known that many gay men never engage in this behaviour.
- Oral sex is practised by lesbian, gay, and heterosexual couples.
- Genital petting and body rubbing is practised by lesbian, gay, and heterosexual couples.
- A further smaller percentage of couples may do no more than caress and kiss.
- Celibacy for some people is natural.

It is known that many couples within all sexualities may from time to time use a variety of these sexual expressions.[2]

2 See:
Hite, Shere, *The Hite Report, Casell* (1976).
Hite, Shere, *The Hite Report on Male Sexuality*, Knopf (1981).

These varied expressions of sexuality, while perhaps contrary to the beliefs of some people, are not restricted by social standing, wealth, poverty or any other category and are spread throughout society.

Finally, it is necessary to keep a sense of perspective when genuinely concerned about paraphilia and hard-core pornography; these behaviours are spread throughout society as a whole, and by population numbers alone are predominantly pursued by heterosexuals.

Such behaviours are a separate issue from a person's basic sexual orientation. It is so easy for the majority and for power-brokers to lay blame on an entire minority as a convenient scapegoat, thus falling to balance the wider reality, which is: that only a percentage of any community within society as a whole participates in these behaviours.

Parkinson, Phil, *The Sex Life of Gay People in NZ – Results of a National Survey*, Lesbian & Gay Resource Centre (1984/5), NZ

CHAPTER EIGHT

Lesbian, Gay, and Bisexual Identity

I want to say clearly that lesbians and gay men have no need to explain their lives, sexuality, or personal feelings. I acknowledge that it is utterly wearying to be continually asked for yet more information by a society which never seems to learn, to hear, or to give equity and justice. Many lesbians and gay men are 'burnt out' from past educative demands. Having worked through the issues and achieved a personally comfortable self-acceptance, the natural wish of most people is to be left in peace to get on with life. Unfortunately there is a continuing need to assist those who are still struggling with the problems of achieving fuller understanding. I sincerely thank those people who felt able yet once more to share of themselves and assist with this text.

Lesbian Identity

Lesbian response was initially difficult to access, their networks being more informal than those of gay men. Lesbians who replied to the questionnaires, and/or whom I contacted personally, contributed wholeheartedly, offering me a generous and caring support which I truly appreciate.

Lesbian Daughters Speak

'My mother seems to think that lesbianism is only sexual activity, she cannot seem to realise that it is a whole way of looking at the world.'

'It has a lot to do with being abused at a young age. It's not a chore to be one of the others! Perhaps too it comes from birth.'

'When I overcame my own fear and denial and 'came out" to my mother, one of her reactions was to share with me her own feelings of love for a woman before she married my father. This allowed her to acknowledge, accept, and validate her own feelings.'

'My partner and I raised her three children together as a couple. They have matured into well balanced, sensible citizens. Each is married now, and one has a daughter of her own.'

'Most lesbians I know, myself included, have spent years doing personal growth work around their sexuality, relationships, biological families and personal insecurities. I am independent physically competent and androgynous. I am discriminated against because of my appearance. I only feel comfortable in jeans and casual clothing. I always knew I was different but not why until I met other dykes.'

'I am a professional woman delighted to be a mother and very much in love with my partner. We own our own home, and have a wide circle of friends. My life feels normal for me. How many other people can say the same?'

'For me it's partially a response to restrictive sex-roles, and finding women more challenging and exciting.'

'It's incredibly frustrating, lonely and horrible to have family and society tell us we are twisted, perverted, abnormal subhumans. The love H. and I have is very strong, equal and to be admired, not pushed down.'

'I believe I am intelligent enough to reject patriarchal priorities that heterosexuals are conditioned to abide by. Our relationship continues to grow with honesty and a loving mutual respect. I am so lucky.'

'The closet is an awful place and nobody should be in there, it is a form of cruelty inflicted by self and others. I am not into separation — it's damaging. Some of my best friends are males both gay and straight.'

'It's a very difficult life, not one I would have "chosen". But I am proud to be lesbian now I have accepted it. Accepting yourself lifts a great burden off your shoulders. I felt so much lighter after I had accepted my sexual orientation.'

'My family is strongly gay. Four out of six kids, and several cousins. Numerous great aunts and uncles suspected, which strongly favours a genetic theory. Certainly nothing in our upbringing that caused it.'

'Certain experiences such as bad times and abuse by men, and good times — friendship and support from women — were part of my decision.'

'(Partly) the behaviour of, and treatment from, my long-term male partner, and (now) dislike of violent males.'

'My upbringing caused me to live a lie of heterosexuality through ten years of marriage.'

These responses to the questionnaires from lesbian daughters on personal 'cause' gave an expected mixture of orientation, abuse, and/or choice. They did not particularly state hatred for men, although for some there was a genuine fear of men, even when not having been personally traumatised. Seeing what had happened to friends and knowing what was happening with incest and unprovoked rapes shaped their feelings of intimacy towards other women. For others the patriarchy which pervades every part of women's lives was felt to be demeaning.

Lesbian Feminists

Lesbian feminists I spoke with asserted the right of women to choose to be lesbian as an expression of intimacy and/or sexuality. However, many parents responding to the questionnaires, whose daughters had made such a choice, found this a difficult perspective to understand.

In an article written in 1988, when the modern feminist

movement had been underway for at least twenty years, Bishop John Shelby Spong commented in *Living in Sin? — a Bishop Rethinks Human Sexuality*:

> *'For centuries sexual attitudes, sexual taboos and sexual practices have been used by dominant groups in society to keep others subordinate. Those who possess power define those who are powerless and impose their own definition on the ones defined. The guiding principle is to ensure the comfort, the convenience, the happiness and the well-being of the dominant ones.'*

This applies particularly to women in society. In the past, many women were forced to marry from economic necessity. Marriages were arranged. Wives were bought, sold and exchanged by men in the open marketplace. Married women could not own property. A husband could spend a woman's inheritance, collect her wages, and leave her destitute. Heterosexuality was compulsory and regulated by the institution of marriage. And these examples still occur in some other countries.

In 'Compulsory Heterosexuality and Lesbian Existence' (1980), Adrienne Rich argued that

> *'Lesbian existence comprises both the breaking of a taboo and the rejection of a compulsory way of life. It is a direct or indirect attack on the male right of access to women.'*

Jenny Rankine, a lesbian-feminist, talked to me about these issues. Later she wrote:

> *'Many lesbians share the experience of discovering that their emotional and sexual feelings were for their own gender, of feeling different and alone, and of eventually identifying as lesbian.*

'I believe, based on talking to many lesbians, that many women who may have feelings for both sexes, or who may not have been previously attracted to women, also choose to identify as lesbians. This has been common in feminist groups around the country and around the western world.

'In my personal experience (when in my late 20s) it took a year or two for my feelings to re-orient from men to women, but after this, sexual identity as a lesbian felt very comfortable for me.

'Lesbian feminists understand the term "compulsory heterosexuality" to describe the way lesbianism is made invisible, or trivialised by the media, schools, laws and other powerful institutions. They argue that oppression of lesbians damages all women. It stops heterosexual women getting too close to their female friends, fearing others will suspect them of lesbianism. It helps to keep women focused on men's needs and in competition with other women. It scares women's from challenging discrimination for fear of being called lesbians as a result.'

Choosing to be Lesbian

Many women have indicated that male abuse has influenced their choice to be lesbian. When one young lesbian says she was raped by a male family member to show her what 'normal' sex was, and that she could 'enjoy it if she tried', and when recent child sexual abuse and incest statistics are causing great concern, would it be surprising if more women did not make such a choice?

However, research on childhood sexual abuse as a cause of later lesbianism is divided in opinion[1] — and many of those choosing to be lesbian have not been the victims of child

1 Finkelhor, David, *Sourcebook on Child Sexual Abuse*, Sage Publications Inc. (1986), USA.

sexual abuse. It cannot be denied that the severe stress and violation of any male sexual abuse, incorporating as it does mental, physical and emotional trauma, makes a compelling argument for the right of choice to be lesbian if so desired.

In Jenny Rankine's words: 'To imply that people don't choose to be homosexual is inaccurate for many lesbians. Many lesbians and heterosexual women have found that their desires for intimacy are fluid and flexible.'

The quotes above show that to be lesbian, whether as a self-styled feminist or not, is a personal fulfilment which is best, right, comfortable and happy. Parents may find this very difficult to understand. Although I can appreciate this, it can be suggested that this reflects parents' own needs rather than those of their daughter. For an adult daughter has the right to choose her own way of life.

Gay Men's Identity

Gay men who responded to the questionnaires and/or whom I contacted personally shared freely of what it means for them to be gay. I am grateful for their kindness and encouragement. They did not view the choice to be gay in the same way that lesbians view choice. Perhaps the reason for this is that for those with a homosexual orientation their gay identity is often acquired slowly, as part of a gradual coming-out process, rather than as a single choice (of course, this is also the case for many lesbians). The forces which lead some women to choose a lesbian identity do not apply in the male case.

Some men in New Zealand who identify as homosexual are not part of a gay community. To be openly a gay man in society is not easy, at least initially, but many said that by being 'out', and growing more confident and self-assertive, they experienced fewer problems in the long run.

Gay Sons Speak

'I cannot feel happy or that I fully accept myself unless I can share this very important part of my life with those who mean so much to me. Do I really have to live two fives? My mother might accept me, but I'm sure my father has no notion of anything other than a heterosexual lifestyle. I'm going to come out to them when feel we all have time to work it through together.'

'My gay friends are as important to me as my family. They are my extended family, and the bonds are very strong.'

'I always knew I was somehow different (NOT quite nice), but didn't know why. My priest advised marriage. Parents should be able to celebrate the differences of their gay children, because it gives them special qualities and makes them special people.'

'It was the appalling, frightening and totally dishonest presentation of the anti-law reform petitions that spurred me into gay politics. This opened my closet door wider and wider. I haven't lost any friends, but rather strengthened many friendships.'

'Was I accepted as a person? No. I felt I had to fight for the same stupid recognition that heterosexuals get automatically. I felt I had to constantly prove myself, argue, and establish an identity so heterosexuals could not deny and dismiss me, as if everything I did was inherently flawed.'

'Being gay makes me who I am, and that's pretty good. If I wasn't gay, I wouldn't be me.'

'In many ways the closer you are to your parents and the more you love them, the harder it is to come out to them, because you risk more. At the same time it's important to do it, so that your parents can relate to you as a real person. It's a terrible dilemma for someone, usually in their late teens, to have to resolve.'

'If someone asks would I prefer to be heterosexual, I say of course not. I have always been homosexual, but I tried to have sexual relationships with women which I perceived as the right thing to do. It was not satisfying or successful. I was twenty-four before I realised what I was doing was not right for me.'

'From very early in primary school I related easier to males than females. Later there were occasions when I attempted suicide. My upbringing enforced a latent homosexuality. During my working life in senior positions I kept very much in the closet, partly from self-denial. Since coming out to my family my second son has not acknowledged this. The rest are supportive. Social, family and boarding school expectations made same-sex orientation completely beyond the pale. It took me over fifty years to acknowledge that I was a homosexual and that it was OK to be so.'

'Part of the problem is that homosexuality simply isn't acknowledged. I want to live a normal life in a loving relationship with a man I love and who will love me; not having to worry about what other people think, to be proud of who we are. I want to be open and not pretend any more in any way at all.'

'I feel each gay man needs to consider being out of the closet more to correct the myths and give role models. It is a personal choice which must be respected if they feel it is safer to stay in the closet.'

'I now teach gay men how to form genuine friendships instead of using and abusing each other. It's hard to believe, but many gay men have never experienced any real friendship. In my opinion one has to come out, get rid of fear, and be a role model in the heterosexual community. That is to join, as any man does, in groups and organisations, not only gay ones ... but this took me years to achieve.'

'We have been together for twelve years; we have, like most couples, had our ups and downs. We are agreed not to go out with others while our relationship is intact. We talk issues over, and are allowed to get angry at each other. We have our "own space" without question, but are honest and trust each other. We have some separate interests, and different jobs.'

'All my friends know about me. If anyone asks I tell them the truth and am lucky if I don't get hurt. I don't act "sissy" or "camp", I'm just me. My lover and myself are having our twenty-fifth anniversary next year. All our friends are couples who have been together over twenty years.'

'I recently came out to my two sons in their twenties. This was traumatic, but because of their love and acceptance it turned into one of the most rewarding moments of my life. My wife and I are divorced, but still friends.'

'We gays don't want tolerance, understanding or compassion, we want love as human beings of equal worth.'

Bisexual Identity

It is not too difficult to gain a perspective of an orientated exclusive homosexuality. Bisexuality, on the other hand, tends to confuse us. It seems lesbians and gay men are apt to infer that such people are in transition to being lesbian or gay, while heterosexual people, misunderstanding the nature of sexual orientation, are inclined to perceive bisexual people are being 'weak, and without self-control'.

Bisexual Daughters and Sons Speak

'If only people would be more open towards others' preference without harassment.' (Son)

'Society forces us to choose between a lesbian, gay or straight identity — any other choice is systematically undermined.' (Daughter)

'I grieve at the non-acceptance which denies our sexuality. This is a great pity as everyone suffers.' (Son)

'The problem is not mine.' (Son)

'I would have been much happier if only one person had said it was OK, healthy, emotionally mature for me to love a man and be loved by a man. This is about emotional attraction and love, more than about sex. There is no such thing as The Gay Lifestyle, we have all kinds of lifestyles and our gayness/ bisexuality is far deeper than any of them.' (Son)

'I have found my friends supportive. I have now come out as a lesbian. I had heterosexual affairs, but found that I can't love men, nor do I wish to share my life with them.' (Daughter)

'When Dad learnt I was bisexual and (now) involved with a woman, he thought it was deliberate to spite him. He was bitter at the probable loss of grandchildren which he saw as some compensation. Ironically, although relationships with men could have made children possible, I have never wanted them. My father blames this entirely on my being bisexual and he will never forgive me. My mother was shocked at first but was mostly concerned for me. We [woman partner and self] are treated as a curiosity, not only do other people think they have the right to offer their opinions and verdicts, but we are expected to be grateful for their advice. It does not occur to them that we like privacy the same as anyone.' (Daughter)

'My wife wants me to be straight. I'm working on it, I don't know if I'll succeed ... so my relationship may fail.' (Son)

'I spent years trying to get family acceptance. Finally I gave up; I also stopped attending church because of this unresolved conflict. I have said accept me as I am. If they cannot, I will no longer have contact with them.' (Son)

These responses demonstrate some difficulty in determining a) whether sexual behaviour with people of both genders means that a person had a bisexual orientation or b) he or she had not always engaged in sexual behaviour congruent with his or her sexual orientation.

Is the married woman who finds herself attracted to another woman bisexually oriented, or has she been socialised into heterosexual behaviour and identity despite a lesbian sexual orientation? In the present environment, it is no wonder that bisexual identity formation is frequently a confused affair.

In *Bisexual Lives* (1988), one contributor commented that far from being promiscuous, most of her life had been spent in celibacy — it being, contrary to common belief, not easy to find a compatible mate. Others said their early years were spent in a succession of eventually failing relationships and trauma, turning from heterosexual to homosexual and back again, before the truth finally dawned that they were in fact bisexual by nature.

When in 1991 the Presbyterian General Assembly discussed the acceptance of homosexual men for ordination, a Presbyterian minister publicly acknowledged his bisexuality and his wife spoke in his support. They had been happily married for twenty-seven years, and had felt it was time to be honest. In their early married life he had been terrified of her discovering his bisexuality because she might leave him. He loved her dearly. Bit by bit he had told her, and eventually there was an understanding of what life was like for him. She says it has not been the centre of their life, just something which has been dealt with from time to time. She accepts his orientation and coming out has brought them even closer together. They received many letters from other couples sharing a similar experience and said obviously there is a great need for information, support and encouragement to work out the issues. (*NZ Woman's Weekly* 9/12/91)

I found and believe human sexuality is a continuum. Just as most people are righthanded, fewer are lefthanded and some are ambidextrous, so too most of us are heterosexual, fewer are homosexual and some are bisexual.

Some bisexual persons can make a loving commitment to one side of the continuum or the other, and, just as a heterosexual man committed to marriage does not place himself at risk with other young women, these too will not place themselves in situations of temptation. I also believe some are unable to do this and may have great difficulty in sustaining a permanent relationship.

When people, frequently after great personal cost, state that a bisexual orientation is for them the only one which can make sense, this should be accepted as their personal truth.

Research in this area is limited, but the information available supports an inherent bisexuality for some people. As it was expressed to me: 'Sexuality is as given and not a matter of choice. How sexuality is acted upon or expressed and selection of sexual partners is largely by choice.'

Who is or is not Homosexual/Bisexual?

The quotes in this chapter clearly establish and explain that being lesbian, gay or bisexual is by personal recognition. Nobody else can say whether someone is or is not homosexual or bisexual.

I believe all adults have the right to the expression of their given sexuality, providing this is consensual and does not hurt, harm or deceive other people. This must be the guideline for us all, whether homosexual, bisexual or heterosexual; ideally our guideline includes honesty, equality and caring in all relationships, together with a well developed, sincere, personal integrity.

It is a shameful indictment of society that many sons and daughters, younger or older, are still misinformed, closeted, afraid and lonely. I hope the perspectives offered in this book will assist them and their parents. Whether lesbian, gay or bisexual, daughters and sons primarily need self-acceptance, and a parental understanding which first and foremost recognises them as individual people.

CHAPTER NINE

Common Parental Fears

Stereotypes

Many of the fears parents have for their lesbian, gay, or bisexual children revolve around stereotypes that have been unconsciously absorbed and come to be believed as factual. Some parents are astounded by their child's disclosure of their sexual orientation because, for instance, they had thought that gay men were all 'effeminate' or that lesbians had 'short hair'. All such stereotyping is wrong.

In the NSW Anti-Discrimination Board study referred to earlier, lesbian and gay respondents included truck-drivers, process workers, steel mill labourers, an ex-priest, an army captain, a policeman, nurses, teachers, and social workers. This diversity is confirmed by my questionnaires for, although not asked, respondents often mentioned their occupation. These were chefs, farmers, psychologists, computer analysts, teachers, nurses, shop assistants, clerks, factory workers and those unemployed.

Many of the fears that parents hold for their children are based on stereotyped ideas about what their lives may hold for them. This chapter discusses one or two of the most pervasive fears based on stereotypes and some of the genuine problems that we can do something about.

Child Molestation

One of the most common and destructive myths surrounding gay men is that they are more inclined to engage in the sexual abuse of children than are heterosexual men. In 1982, the New South Wales Anti-Discrimination Board conducted a major review of all the information they could find on the topic, but found no evidence at all to support this contention. Most children who are sexually abused are girls, and they are abused by heterosexual men; even in the cases of boys who have been sexually abused, most of the abusers identified as heterosexual. Sexual attraction to children is called paedophilia. Many paedophiles are sexually attracted to both female and male children.

I contacted Helen Packard of the Auckland HELP Foundation, and also spoke with Stephen Jacobs, an independent counsellor, on this matter. They concurred that New Zealand's experience corresponds with the reports available from abroad, which estimate that ninety-seven per cent of offenders against young boys are heterosexual in orientation.

Stephen Jacobs commented that in eight years of working with some 200 sex offenders and/or paedophiles, he had seen only two cases (i.e. in this case one per cent) of such men being homosexually orientated. I believe, therefore, that it is reasonable to surmise that any research on the abuse of boys in New Zealand will follow overseas findings. And abuse of our children, girls and boys, will prove to be almost exclusively by heterosexual males.

In July 1994 study based on 269 cases of child abuse, researchers at the University of Colorado reported (in the Journal of American Academy of Pediatrics) that only two of the offenders were gay or bisexual. They concluded a child's risk of molestation by a parent's heterosexual partner or by a relative was over 100 times greater than being abused by a non-heterosexual.

A Childless (and Grandchildless) Future

Children are not assured from any relationship. Infertility is a problem for an estimated ten per cent of couples, and many young marrieds defer having children or do not choose to have any. A lesbian daughter who wants a child may conceive by artificial insemination, and a gay son may well be a donor by arrangement (see Chapter 13). Many lesbians and gays have children by a former marriage. Alternatively, while adoption and fostering are difficult, they are not impossible. It should not be assumed that all gay and lesbian people do not want to have children, or do not have children, any more than it can be assumed that all heterosexual people do want children.

If, as a parent of a childless lesbian daughter or gay son, you yearn to be a grandparent, may I suggest that there are already many children needing affection. For instance, you might join a hospital grandparents' group, to visit little ones who are ill and away from home, or befriend a young family with no grandparents of their own nearby. It may not feel quite the same, but it is well known that in helping others we also comfort ourselves.

A Lonely Future

Parents often fear their homosexual daughters and sons will be lonely, particularly as they grow older This is no more true for them than for your other children Many will live in long-term relationships, enjoy their own children or the company of nieces and nephews, or develop a second 'lesbian or gay family' for support and friendship. No one, heterosexual or homosexual, can guarantee their relationship will be a lifelong partnership, produce children, or that a partner will not suffer an untimely death.

Daughters and sons will be better able to sustain long-term relationships if the conflicts and non-acceptance of their sexuality at home (and in society) are minimal, and if their self-esteem is strong and well supported.

Self-destructive Behaviours

Gay men and lesbian women are known to have higher incidences of substance abuse and suicide (see below) than their heterosexual counterparts. It needs to be stressed, however, that this results not from being gay or lesbian, but from the low self-esteem arising from the responses of others to a gay or lesbian orientation. Further, this low self-esteem is not experienced just by those who disclose their sexual orientation to others. Lesbians and gay men do not disclose their sexual orientation because they fear the negative reactions of others; sadly, this fear can have the same debilitating consequences as the negative reactions feared.

Substance Abuse

Overseas research, particularly in the United States, has shown very high rates of substance abuse in the lesbian and gay communities, but New Zealand statistics are sparse. Many people spoke to me of their concern over these problems. A counsellor for the New Zealand AIDS Foundation's Awhina Centre in Wellington says:

> *'It is not uncommon for young men to admit to us, of using drugs, or whatever [substance] to dull the pain of coming to terms with their sexuality, and that whilst affected by this, to having placed themselves in a situation where they risked becoming HIV positive.'*

In the New Zealand study 'Lesbians Like Us' (1988)[1] of fifty-seven self-selected lesbians, sixty per cent said they had drunk to excess occasionally, and fourteen per cent said they regularly drank more than they should. The researchers con-

1 Report No.6 Tamaki Makaurau 'Lesbians Like Us: the place of alcohol in the lives of New Zealand Women', Anthropology Dept. University of Auckland, 1986.

cluded that because lesbians frequently faced hostility and discrimination from those closest to them, it was not surprising that they should turn to alcohol as a means of escape.

Substance abuse can also involve food. Over or under-eating can be an expression of non-acceptance of self. In *The New Loving Someone Gay*, Don Clark argues that many lesbians and gay men need to 'reclaim' their bodies. As he sees it, some gay men and lesbians may 'disown' their bodies in a number of different ways:

- by tuning out and ignoring the body as a vague nuisance used to transport mind and spirit

- by taking revenge on it, e.g. by causing it to have repeated accidents and illnesses, or simply by overfeeding or under-feeding it

- by reconstruction — including excessive body-building exercise and redecoration to obscure — or by hiding it in a facade that looks just like the 'perfect' people in the advertisements.

He believes that these are all ways in which the gay man or lesbian (and indeed many heterosexual people) reframe their body as 'it— not me'. Clark also suggests ways to help oneself get rid of anti-body feelings.

It was mentioned to me by several lesbians and gay men that if a young person has been brought up to believe homosexual expression is dirty, disgusting or perverted, repulsion of bodily needs can be a means of coping. Anorexia nervosa or bulimia can become an unarticulated 'cry for help' or an 'acceptable' form of self-destruction. Compulsive behaviours (which are frequently allied to depression) may be experienced in many ways. And imposed or personal denial of sexual orientation may bring compulsive sexual needs or behaviours which have a risk of becoming addictive.

The Suicide Risk

New Zealand has one of the highest suicide rates in the world for those aged fifteen to twenty-five years. Barry Taylor, a senior advisory officer at the Ministry of Youth Affairs, and this country's foremost authority on youth suicide, says many of these young people are lesbian or gay. He firmly states that New Zealand needs to deal urgently with this problem by recognising that a significant proportion of the population is not heterosexual, and signalling that gay, lesbian, and bisexual people are valued equally with heterosexual people.

Recent studies from the University of Minnesota show nearly one in three young American homosexual men attempt suicide. No single reason for this was given, but researchers said the would-be suicides recognised themselves as homosexuals at an early age, and apparently could not cope with this and society's homophobic pressures.

In the United States, the Secretary's Taskforce on Youth Suicide (1989) emphasised that the difficulties of forming and retaining relationships, when these are not validated by society and also conflict with family, are factors in lesbian and gay youth suicide. It said:

> *'Family problems are probably the most significant factor in youth suicide. Youth derive their core sense of being cared about and belonging from their families. Gay youth may make suicide attempts after being rejected by their families. For gay and lesbian youth forced to leave home, the loss of parental love and support remains a critical issue for them.'*

The report says that gay and lesbian youth face more verbal and physical abuse from family members and harassment than other youth. They may hide their orientation from their parents out of fear of rejection and of not meeting family expectations of heterosexual marriage and having children. A religion that defines homosexuality as sinful, and a family that makes homophobic remarks can add to an insupportable burden and an attempted or, sadly, a completed suicide may result:

> *'They remain unaware of the variety of positive adult gay lifestyles available to them ... They may engage in increasingly reckless and self-destructive behaviour as an expression of the sadness and anger they feel over unresolved issues with families and despair over their new life ... A suicide attempt may result from a negative contact with their family, the breaking up with a lover, or failure to make it on their own.'*

My questionnaires showed that forty of 103 gay and/or bisexual men, and eight of forty-three lesbian and/or bisexual women had attempted or considered suicide. Sixty-five gay men and twenty lesbian women personally knew a gay man, lesbian, or bisexual person who had committed suicide. Not all of these were young people, and a few deaths were attributed to despair over HIV, and/or the illness of AIDS, but Barry Taylor's comments in the Youth Mental Health Project discussion paper on 'Gay & Lesbian Youth Services in New Zealand' (1989) are still relevant:

> *'These difficulties stem not from the [young person's] sexual orientation but society's unacceptance. If we are to be successful in suicide prevention we must take steps to ensure that a more supportive and accepting society is created where young lesbians and gays are accepted and affirmed in their sexual identity.'*

I believe parents have a part to play in this. The re-educating of society is our responsibility as much as it is that of any other interested group.

Suicide Warning Signs

There are warning signs that indicate a person may be suicidal. Please note that one or two of these warning signs by themselves do not necessarily indicate a potential suicide, but several in combination could suggest a serious problem in a person's life which could lead to a suicide attempt. Barry Taylor says the signs to watch for are:

- a preoccupation with themes of death or expression of suicidal thoughts
- a wish to give away prized possessions
- lingering feelings of failure
- sudden drops in school marks or truancy
- withdrawal from friends and family
- increased use of alcohol or drugs
- personality changes such as outbursts of anger, reckless behaviour, or apathy about health and appearance.

What Can We Do?

If you become concerned for someone, thinking they are showing signs which may be pointing to a suicide attempt, encourage them to talk to you or to a person they will trust. Seek their cooperation for you to arrange professional counselling for them; offer to go with them and support them.

However, should you recognise a person is approaching suicidal crisis point and is at immediate risk, it is important to get help at once (preferably with their consent) from a professional they/you can trust, such as their/your doctor, or an agency such as Lifeline. Meanwhile, it is most necessary to have someone stay with them and provide caring support.

HIV/AIDS

The nightmare which haunts many parents, particularly those of gay sons, is HIV infection and the development of AIDS this may bring. The following information has been supplied by the New Zealand AIDS Foundation educators.

Who gets AIDS and how does this happen? HIV, the virus which eventually causes AIDS, is not caught by being gay, or from sharing cups or cutlery, coughing, sneezing, touching or kissing. In fact, because it is a fragile virus, it is actually very difficult to catch.

The blood, semen, or vaginal fluids of an infected person must find a way into another person's bloodstream for them to become infected. This could happen directly by blood transfusion (before New Zealand started to screen the blood supply), for example, or less directly through cuts or sores or a few types of specialised cells which are found inside the body.

The main ways in which the HIV has been transmitted have been through sexual intercourse (both vaginal and anal) and through injecting drug users sharing needles and syringes. In New Zealand recorded transmission to date has shown to be mainly through homosexual anal intercourse, although anyone, male or female, who engages in unsafe sexual behaviour with a person who has the HIV is at risk.

The World Health Organization (WHO) carefully monitors the HIV/AIDS situation globally and in its press release No.9 of 12/2/92 says: 'Worldwide well over 90% of newly infected adults acquired their infection from heterosexual sexual intercourse. This reflects the continuing trend towards heterosexual transmission of the [HIV] virus seen not only in developing countries but increasingly in the industrialised world.' New Zealand therefore cannot become complacent or relax its vigilance in education or in the provision of health services.

It is important to remember that if your son is gay or bisexual this does not necessarily put him at risk from HIV. There are many other sexual acts between men which are completely safe and even anal intercourse can be made much safer by using condoms with a water-based lubricant.

Female-to-female transmission of the HIV infection is very difficult. Where cases have been claimed, other routes of infection have not been ruled out.

AIDS Education

Besides keeping yourself safe, you can help to educate others about AIDS.

If you have teenagers, it is your duty to be literate on HIV/AIDS and educate them. Telling them to say 'No' to sexual activity, or using threats, is not sufficient or realistic. If you are a grandparent, your grandchildren may respond to your love and education better than to that of their parents.

You can help to ensure that the local high school Board of Trustees implements anti-discriminatory sexuality education into its main syllabus — for the sake of not only teenagers, but for the whole community. (One high school in Whangarei reduced an average of four or five teenage pregnancies a year to none in 1991 by using a consistent programme of education, combined with social skills awareness and good support systems.)

If you are an employee, or an employer, you can ensure that your workplace is informed and educated, that there are anti-discrimination practices in place for homosexuals or their family members, with an emergency accident code of procedure established for all men and women regarding

HIV/AIDS.

If you are a teenager you can spread accurate HIV/AIDS information among your friends and ask your school for class teaching from the NZ Family Planning Association, NZ AIDS Foundation, or Te Roopu Tautoko Trust educators. It is not responsible to risk your own or someone else's life. It is not acceptable to bully or tease lesbian or gay schoolmates for any reason.

If you are a health professional — doctor, dentist, nurse, or therapist — you can ensure safe codes of practice for clients, staff, and yourself.

HIV/AIDS and Parents

There were several poignant accounts in the questionnaires returned to me and in letters received from anguished parents, whose sons are HIV positive, dying, or, sadly, had died from AIDS:

> 'Our son is only twenty-three years old, he went to Australia, he is now HIV positive. Not wanting to hurt us, it was five months before he told us. We wondered why the letters had stopped. We both went and stayed with the parents of one of his friends. They've been coping with the same thing longer than us. It was helpful to share their experience, especially for the fathers. Our whole family had counselling at the AIDS Foundation when we heard the news and they were really helpful but not all his sisters are coping. Sometimes I try to "switch off" and hope things will all go away, they don't of course, and then I feel guilty for feeling like that I can't emphasise enough the terrible feelings we went through when we heard the news but we know truly that we love our son very much.'

> 'Our son in Australia has AIDS and probably has not more than a year to live. Our love for him is not diminished, but we know that unless he rejects and turns away from this lifestyle, he will have no place in God's Kingdom.'

'When my son died, the adverse reactions from close friends and relations was something I've taken a long time to come to terms with. He lived in Australia and it wasn't until he was dying that he told us. I wish so much I had known sooner that he was gay.'

'Please accept your children as they are, life is too short to be bitter. I have found gay people are kind, deeply caring people, good fun and eager to get the best from life. I regard my son's friends as among my best friends even though he has now died from AIDS.'

'My son in Australia is dying from AIDS, and I have cancer. Neither of us can travel, so we make do with what toll calls we can afford.'

'My worst fear has been realised He told us two years ago that he has HIV. He is in Australia.'

It will be noted nearly all the quotes are from parents whose sons are in Australia. With its larger cities, Australia has for decades been a mecca for young New Zealanders fleeing the anti-gay discrimination of society in general and family at home.

The AIDS epidemic was well under way in the bigger Australian cities before worldwide awareness of the disease became evident. New Zealand had more warning, so some prevention and support systems were in place ahead of the first cases here.

The stigma and secrecy surrounding HIV/AIDS in New Zealand is like that attached to cancer, illegitimacy, or asthma in years gone by. It is a factor in some young, and some not so young, New Zealanders still denying to themselves the possibilities of infection. When depressed, confused, or under the influence of alcohol or other drugs (whether here or overseas), nothing seems to matter and caution may be thrown away in at-risk behaviours.

The New Zealand AIDS Foundation's booklet Living with

HIV: a Personal Handbook explains that those who love and care for people who are positive tested HIV (or are AIDS developed) also go through the same strains, stresses, and emotional see-sawing experienced by those who are unwell:

> *'You may experience stages of shock and grief similar to those the person you love is going through. Don't try to suppress your fears, or anger, or doubts about how you will cope. It's far better to express them to people who can help you.'*

Surely few parents will reject a child who is fatally ill? Sadly this has been known to happen. On the other hand, some families are being cruelly stigmatised and ostracised because of their association with their dying children. To protect themselves or others, these families feel they must not ask for, or receive, the help they desperately need from their extended family, friends or neighbours.

Some families, although appearing to accept their ill sons, do not allow brothers, sisters or family members to visit or touch them, to give the love and comfort they deserve and need. It is essential that clear information on HIV/AIDS be more widely spread so that common sense can eradicate misguided ignorance.

Everyone can help to break down discrimination, fear and stereotyping about AIDS. As one way to do this, the NZAF advises, with acknowledgement to Peter Scott's *The National AIDS Manual* (UK 1990), these suggestions for avoiding hurtful language:

- 'Talk about — "people/person living with HIV" or "people with AIDS" not "AIDS victims, sufferers, patients or cases".'
- 'Terms such as "innocent victims" imply guilty ones, usually those who contracted HIV from sex or sharing

needles. Everyone has a right to express their sexuality and there are very few people who use no drugs at all. Everyone who has HIV has it by accident.'

- 'It is important to emphasise the activities through which HIV is transmitted, and not blame groups of people.'

- 'The use of terms like AIDS "sufferers, victims, patients, or cases" rather than "HIV positive people" portrays them as "doomed, helpless, dependent, passive, or somehow deserving illness".'

- 'The term "general public" when talking of AIDS is usually used to mean non-homosexual and non drug-using people. It implies that these people are not part of the public and don't count, or are a threat to the general public. Using "heterosexuals" or the "whole population" is better.'

Fear and discrimination will not disappear until there is consistent, widespread education to reduce ignorance and prejudice. Legislation is urgently required to protect people living with HIV/AIDS, and particularly gay or bisexual men from discriminatory practices. Otherwise those most needing tests for HIV will not be prepared to have them, and the spread of infection will not be halted. The bigoted who call for 'registration' of those who are HIV/AIDS positive are simply driving HIV/AIDS underground and putting the next generation at risk.

Other Sexually Transmitted Diseases

ALL sexual activity, penetrative or oral, needs protection against STDs (see glossary). This applies equally whether male or female — straight, bisexual, lesbian or gay. Advice regarding the use and purchase of dental dams or condoms is available through Family Planning Clinics, Sexual Health Centres, the NZ AIDS Foundation or pharmacies.

CHAPTER TEN

Homophobia and Discrimination

Take some time before you read on, and try to answer each of these questions (which are adapted from a Family Life Educator Journal):

How would I define heterosexuality?

How could I tell if someone was heterosexual?

What causes heterosexuality?

Is it possible that heterosexuality stems from a neurotic fear of others of the same sex?

Heterosexual people are often portrayed as being preoccupied with sex. Are they really?

When did I last see heterosexual people flaunt their sexuality?

In a heterosexual couple, who takes the dominant role and who takes the passive role?

The divorce rate for married couples is escalating. Why do heterosexual people seem to find it so difficult to stay in long-term relationships?

Ninety-nine per cent of rapists are reported to be heterosexual.

Why are heterosexual men so sexually aggressive?

Ninety-seven per cent of child molesters are reported to be heterosexual. Is it safe to expose children to heterosexual teachers, scout leaders, sports coaches, etc?

When did I choose my sexual orientation?

How easy would it be for me to change my sexual orientation, starting right now?

What have been your reactions to answering these questions? What feelings have you experienced? You will have realised these are the reverse of questions, statements and expectations commonly aimed at homosexual people.

In *Society and the Healthy Homosexual* (1975), Dr George Weinberg argued that anti-homosexual attitudes and behaviour, namely 'homophobia', comprised a debilitating personality problem in those who hold such attitudes. Homophobia in society, as is explained later, has many adverse consequences for gay men, lesbians and their families.

In general, homophobia is still prevalent in New Zealand, where pioneering stoicism, physical strength, macho-sporting endeavour and macho-sexual superiority are glorified. Nor is bigotry dead. Although it can be said that today homophobia is slowly being countered by better education, parents worry greatly, with good reason, about the attitudes of society towards their lesbian, gay or bisexual children.

It is equally hard for many parents to accept that they have been (or are) an unthinking part of a society which condemns homosexuality and bisexuality, without making any distinctions. It is natural to want to defend our own heterosexuality and most difficult to make the leap of perception which enables us to understand another person's sexual orientation.

Most people do not express their homophobia in physical ways, but regardless of whether an expression of prejudice is subtle or overt, it is the accumulation of homophobic and bigoted pressures which, as the questionnaire responses and letters to me showed:

- Affects the sense of self-identity and self-esteem in those at whom it is directed, and produces in them a rejection of self, or of others.

- Produces a sub-culture of closed socialising and friendships, and eventually in some a closeted 'ghetto' mentality.

In an article, 'Homophobia: Scientists find clues to its roots' (*New York Times*, 1990), Daniel Goldman reported:

> *'A rise in hostile actions against homosexuals can be traced primarily to hatred based on fear and self-righteousness, in which homosexuals are perceived as contemptible threats to the moral universe, rather than to the AIDS epidemic ... new findings confirm that some men use hostility and violence towards homosexuals to reassure themselves about their own sexuality ... in America about three-quarters of homosexuals say they have been harassed by people calling them names, and as many as one in four say they have been physically assaulted ... homophobia [relates to] ... the stereotypic perception: the more feminine a gay man appears, the more hostility [and anxiety] he evokes in other men ... in insecure heterosexual women, a lesbian can arouse fears of their own latent homosexual feelings and arouse hostility ...'*

Expressions of Prejudice

What, I wondered, was the situation in New Zealand regarding discrimination, violence, and harassment?

Generally, I have found those people in their later twenties, their thirties or forties to be more at ease with, and have more understanding of, homosexuality than older people. Yet I have also heard of strong discrimination, particularly among younger teenagers.

My questionnaires showed that of the gay and bisexual sons, sixty four out of 103, well over half, had strongly felt or received direct discrimination. This is what they reported:

> 'My partner's car was smashed with a sledgehammer, police would do nothing, we had to move. Told to leave my church.'
>
> 'We had to leave our church — what damage would we do? I now go to a church where there's love for all, old or young. I am very happy there.'
>
> 'The police stopped me walking arm-in-arm with a man; was stopped and questioned because I wore a sarong.'
>
> 'From former wife's new husband — highly abusive phone calls and mail.'
>
> 'My boss considered me inferior because I was "queer".'
>
> 'I was refused a flat because I'm openly gay.'
>
> 'Neighbours who prefer not to speak; possibly in work promotion I am not sure; name calling in the street.'
>
> 'Taunts when out socially; definitely refused one job because I am gay, although the best qualified.'
>
> 'I lost my job after a fight — I'd been called a "poof".'
>
> 'I'm facing dismissal from my work/career because of being openly gay.'
>
> 'Primary and secondary school were hell. They obviously knew it before I did!'
>
> 'Teasing and isolation at secondary school, beatings by staff and prefects. I am very cautious and avoid conflict.'

Two men reported being picked on and beaten in the street without provocation, for being 'feminine' in general appearance. Another was thrown out of a bar for the same reason. Many gay men were harassed in public venues.

Thirty-six out of forty-three, over two-thirds, of lesbian or bisexual daughters had strongly felt or directly received discrimination. This is what they reported:

'I've been spat at in the street, kicked out of a pub, verbal abuse, and obscene phone calls. Was denied information and literature on lesbianism in general.'

'Lost some straight friends; partner not invited to family gatherings.'

'My partner's boss was very derogatory at a work "do", he eventually kicked in the door of her car.'

'People in the community make jokes about me; am never asked how my partner is; a landlord who spread gossip because I was late with my rent — the only time in three years — he wouldn't have minded if I wasn't lesbian.'

'My relationship isn't recognised like those of my straight brothers and sisters.'

'I have to do the job better, work harder, than male co-workers.'

'Evicted when my landlord found out; foster mother doesn't want to know me anymore; usual giggles, sneers and snide remarks at work.'

'Being patronised; my right to be on a Women's Health Committee was challenged by a male (of course!) due to my sexuality.'

'My lover and I had our lives threatened by her brother-in-law. First he molested us, then physically attacked us and later fired shots at our house. The police would not take it seriously as he said we made love in front of his children! We were forced to leave the area.'

'It's hard to find work if you are positive and "out", although they say who I sleep with is my business they don't like my "strange radical ideas" about: feminism — the oppression of women; racism — support for the Treaty of Waitangi; men — that I don't necessarily want to socialise with them.'

'It's the assumptions that I'm single and looking for a man; that a woman is incomplete without a man; that I'm a threat!'

'Yelled at and harassed in the street, at the movies, in hotels.'

'I feel safe in my family and at work, but am anxious and fearful in public. I would dearly love to be myself.'

'I was beaten up by a man who fancied my lover; spat on by men; at work — lewd comments, "queer" jokes, graphic drawings of male genitals on my toilet walls, loss of promotion; terrible assumptions about lesbians by the medical professionals.'

'My professional credibility has been questioned; I cannot give my partner the benefit of my nationality, nor upon my death leave her my goods and property as of right; I cannot visit or work in some countries which restricts my career; I was raped by a man but the police inferred a lesbian couldn't be raped!'

'Refused a flat; refused a change from night shift, as day shift would put me in contact with "young girls"; a complaint to DSW made about me, because my three year old son was "morally at risk" — my partnership was five years old and happy, and my son was happy.'

'The double standard — it's okay to be lesbian, but not to live like one.'

These responses from lesbian, gay or bisexual daughters and sons were repeated many times with variations. The unending homophobic rude remarks, innuendos, actual or perceived threats of abusive behaviour from others, unreliable support from those in authority, and the inability to be oneself in many situations is wearying, hurtful and incredibly destructive to self-esteem.

There are constant put-clowns, jokes and comments. Often I have been confronted with 'What a pity "they" have spoilt the use of the word "gay" '. However, the misuse of the original meanings of such words as queen, faggot, poof, queer, dyke or fairy does not seem to be such a problem! I was given several explanations as to how the word 'gay' came to be synonymous with homosexuality but none could be conclusively verified. The one I liked best was that it is an acronym for Good As You!

The more obviously androgynous a person is, the worse it becomes. Both men and women have said that although passing as straight they felt forced to hide, play it cool, and not anger their family, boss, workmates, church or the authorities by being openly themselves. Such stress greatly affects their well-being.

These people are not speaking of explicit sexual or overt behaviour. This is not even holding hands, looking lovingly, walking arm-in-arm, taking a lover to social occasions, or daring to share accommodation with her/him. It is the non-recognition — especially in smaller townships or country areas — of these rights which heterosexuals take for granted that understandably hurts. Added to this is the frequent denial of rights to equal opportunity in employment, housing, legal issues, long-term partnerships, custody, insurance, church membership and more.

It hurts us deeply as families when we hear our loving, law-abiding children thoughtlessly or deliberately denigrated. We have been great keepers of secrets, fearing for theirjobs, social status, safety and even their very lives. Some parents who wrote to me had never before (in one case over twenty-three years) told anyone that their child was homosexual. Others dared not sign their names to letters or questionnaires because they lived in small communities and feared recognition. Elderly parents of a bisexual son who died from AIDS felt they could not tell anyone of this to protect their small grandchildren, thus adding to their own sorrow and stress by denying themselves needed support.

There are many stressful situations of 'referred homophobia' experienced by parents, siblings, and children of lesbians and gay men. They are sensitive to and flinch from the slights and abuse aimed at homosexuals and bisexuals which reflect on their loved family members. They know and fear that they will receive discrimination and abuse from the bigoted and homophobic. They fear ostracism for themselves from other family or friends. Initially this adds to their upset feelings. They need information before they can come out, and confront their own and others' homophobia with assurance.

Is it any wonder that sometimes, after decades of peacefully working for recognition, our daughters and sons become involved in militant activism? Then the self-righteous say, 'Look at them, we cannot encourage this!'

Discrimination in Employment

Arguably the greatest area of concern regarding discrimination is employment. This applies particularly to work for young people and in traditional trades which are seen as 'macho' for men or as unfeminine and 'butch' for women. The following excuses for non-employment and 'employment myths' are taken from the report of the NSW Anti-Discrimination Board Report:

- more than one spells trouble
- other employee prejudice
- public and/or client prejudice
- poor work performance
- effeminacy or aggro-butch
- fear they will flaunt it
- security and/or blackmail problems.

Lesbians, gay men and bisexuals have a right to equal opportunity in employment — and not through thinly veiled hostility or open ridicule, but with a genuine recognition that their sexuality, although different from that of others, should be treated with equal respect and consideration. Of course, this does not mean the right (nor do they want it) to overtly express their sexuality in a manner inappropriate to the workplace. It means that any friendly discussion of private lives be the same as for heterosexuals.

'Outing'

Many lesbians and gay men fear their more radically 'out' peers. With some reason, they fear being 'outed or sprung', for assault and reprisals may follow. It is their right to remain closeted. A person may not feel discriminated against if 'out' to family and friends who count most to them. It is a dilemma, because younger ones do need examples of caring partnerships and of successful good citizenship, from those in all walks of life, but good role models are not secured by 'outing'.

Combating Homophobia

Homophobic discrimination is often used to cover up the embarrassment, loathing, fear or anxiety heterosexual people (and some homosexual people) feel because they have not confronted their beliefs. It is not easy to confront these beliefs, because we have been conditioned for generations as a society to accept them with little questioning.

Parents can consider:

- Complaining against those who do not give their daughters and sons equal rights — e.g. insurers; medical, legal, dental and other groups or practitioners; and those who circulate homophobic material in radio and television programmes, or in print.

- Lobbying for support programmes and funding.

- By-passing those schools which do not teach anti-discrimination, or supply inclusive sexuality education.

- Lobbying members of parliament and government departments on the issues of health, housing, employment, education, justice and social welfare.

- Employing or patronising only those firms or organizations who are not discriminatory, or are actively supportive.

I believe that as parents, together with our lesbian, gay and bisexual daughters and sons, we need to stand together on these issues. The size of our united lobby is quite sufficient to ensure the provision of equal rights and anti-discrimination laws if any further action for these is required, or to ensure their enforcement when they are enacted.

CHAPTER ELEVEN

A Religious Dilemma?

For parents holding deep convictions on biblical and/or denominational views of homosexuality, to discover a daughter or son is lesbian, gay or bisexual is profoundly disturbing. I understand this. For over thirty years I was active in church attendance, church groups and bible study classes. Christianity became an important part of my life. Tending to believe what I had been taught without too much question, those things I could not quite agree with I ignored, telling myself that no church could be perfect.

In the 1980s, largely through severe illness, together with becoming aware in 1987 that our son was gay, I both rebuilt and rethought many aspects of my life. This included a reassessment of my being a Christian and my denominational allegiance.

To date I have read over one hundred books, articles and reports relating to aspects of lesbianism, gayness and bisexuality — many of which are the very latest findings. I found that scientific, biological, sociological and psychological evidence is of the strong opinion that sexual orientation (whether heterosexual, homosexual, or bisexual) is not something which can be 'changed'.

On the other hand, I had been taught that the Bible condemns 'homosexuality'. How could my religious beliefs be incorporated with the new things I had learnt? To debate the biblical/ religious dilemma is difficult. It seems necessary to attempt this here because I believe it is important — not only for Christian parents, their daughters and sons, but for all who hold strong Christian beliefs. The findings and comments given will I hope be enlightening, stimulating further search of the scriptures. To enable this search for truth, prejudice must be laid aside and the verses studied in their original context of history, race, and specific needs of the times.

Other People's Experiences

First let us look at the questionnaire responses on religious/ biblical issues from parents, daughters and sons. Then the reconciling view from some overseas and New Zealand bible scholars and church leaders, who are qualified to supply insights, will be presented.

What Parents Said

The question to parents was — 'Does your own religious or the biblical view of homosexuality make it difficult for you to accept your daughter or son's sexuality? If Yes", please explain.' These are some of their replies:

'I had a strict "white, anglo-saxon, Protestant upbringing". All sexuality was seen as sinful, or not to be enjoyed.'

'I can no longer belong to any church that will not accept my son as it does me.'

'I believe in a loving God, as long as we live a good life God loves us whoever we are.'

'My church says same-sex acts are not normal. I say it's a natural difference.'

'My God is large in Love… He is the only judge.'

'He was accepted in my church, now they will not recognise his goodness and integrity rather than his sexuality. Yet Christ's love for all is unconditional.'

'Initially it affected me, but many Christians have double standards in sexuality.'

'God created male and female to be together, wrong sexual relationships are condemned. God's word is unchangeable and secure.'

'The Bible condemns same gender sex; God did not intend people should live this way.'

'As a Catholic it is against all I was taught.'

'My two lesbian daughters were excommunicated from the Mormon Church.'

'No, but religious bigotry by those who know little about it makes me angry.'

Some parents who belonged to Roman Catholic, Bahai, or Mormon churches and to the Salvation Army, felt that they could not mention a daughter or son's homosexuality in their church fellowship, which saddened them. Others had received rejection for doing so, which caused them to radically review the church in question. A few parents found love and support in such denominations. Of course, experience varied from congregation to congregation.

What Daughters and Sons Said

What they said illustrates the effects of many of these judgements or views:

- Strong unyielding attitudes of Fundamentalist, Baptist, Protestant and Roman Catholic teaching had caused heartache and family rifts — they felt unloved and rejected.
- Messages of psychotherapy and/or medicine, now obsolete, are still believed. These 'immature or neurotic' theories equate to the 'sinful or wicked' or 'deliberate choice' beliefs of outdated religious attitudes.
- The religious background to society's behaviour, morality, and laws still prohibits acceptance of homosexuality in general. This influence is out of all proportion to actual religious observance nationally.
- Their own beliefs from assimilated teaching and/or atti-

tudes have meant long struggles to accept themselves, delaying the coming-out process (by up to fifty years in one case) or in sad attempts to many and deny the reality (in several instances it was over twenty years before this was resolved).

- The imposed guilt; the enforced low self-esteem; the grief of family; rejection by family or friends; the discomfort generally with sex and/or sexuality which is seen as sinful and/or dirty, whether homosexual or heterosexual — all amounted to a 'terrible' burden.

- It meant their questioning if God still accepted them; as a teenager being given no other options; the family message was that homosexuals were 'sick' and that women only marry men.

- They were brought up as 'good, pure, normal' heterosexuals without any thought that they might be otherwise.

Some daughters and sons reported that they were later accepted by parents who had thought through their beliefs. Other daughters and sons believed that God who made all things 'found His creation good' and therefore loves them unconditionally. Some lesbians, gays and their parents now worship God in the Metropolitan Community Church[1], where they receive total love, support and acceptance. The problem here is that if this is encouraged, other churches would be seen as the priest (in Christ's story of the Good Samaritan) who 'passed by on the other side of the road'. Instead many are, like the Levite in the story, opting for 'half-way' by saying 'we will love homosexuals as people, but not countenance any expression of their sexuality'. (Although of course every church has diversity in its membership and not every member subscribes to this approach.)

---

1 The two largest gay organisations in the world are the MCC and the Gay Christian Movement.

What Do the Churches Say?

While many mainline churches remain officially opposed to homosexuality, there is a new spirit abroad and many are earnestly debating the issues and have lesbian and gay support groups. A number of significant statements by individuals have been made in the last two or three years. Dr Felix Donnelly in his address to the National Gay Christian Conference in Auckland 1991 said:

> *'The sanctions against homosexuals endorsed by Christian churches are by and large the product of ignorant, fearful assumptions from a culture that had many unhealthy feelings of shame and guilt, as well as myths about things sexual ... In terms of creation, God actually created the homosexual as much as God has created the heterosexual. To deny the reality of one's sexuality is to deny in essence the Creator's plan ... [And speaking of consensual adult homosexuality said] It needs to be stressed that:*
>
> - *one's sexuality is not of one's choosing*
> - *what is important is one's integrity and honesty in conforming to guidelines that the person believes are authentic for their sexual direction*
> - *it is the basic right for all, including Christians, to be able to love and love fully, including expressions of intimacy; and*
> - *your own conscience is your ultimate guide towards authenticity as a Christian*
> - *one should explore the ways which, as a homosexual, one can grow and love through an acceptance of oneself, through concern for the one loved, and through commitment to expressing that love with tenderness and responsibility and caring.'*

The Right Reverend Bruce Gilberd, Anglican Bishop of Auckland, in his address to the Third Session of the Forty-sixth Synod 1991 (p.7) said:

> *'My present firm view is that it is appropriate to recognise gay men and lesbian women as full participants in the Church. Some of these will be celibate, some are faithful in relationships, some will be exploring relationships, just as heterosexual persons do. After all we affirm that the Church is for all people ... A dialogue, open debate, in respect and love is what moves us all towards life-giving truth. Justice requires this also ...'*

A former Moderator of the Presbyterian General Assembly, the Right Reverend John Murray, expressed a personal view when reflecting on human rights. He said:

> *'No one should be discriminated against on the grounds of sexuality.' [And, on ordination:] 'I stand firmly on the ground that the issue should be only whether one can be an effective minister of the Gospel.'*
> (*Northern Advocate* 20/7/9 1)

In a letter to me in July 1991 he said: 'My position has been to try and bring understanding and reconciliation between heterosexuals and homosexuals in the Church.'

Some mainstream churches are offering lesbian, gay, and bisexual Christians limited church membership or have established specific support groups for them. For the mainline churches, as they become more inclusive, a stumbling block will be the individual man-made theologies (studies of God's nature and purposes) and doxologies (liturgies, forms of worship, hymns) which are strongly interwoven with heterosexual and patriarchal influence.

With a spirit of willingness and reconciliation these could be adjusted with Christian love. For example, it is interesting to note that people are not 'married' by the church. The church officiates weddings under licence to perform the state legal requirements, to which it adds its own blessings and customs. There is effectively no bar to loving, faithful lesbian and gay partnerships being blessed by the church. This would both support and help to cement their commitment.

There are religious-based groups, from both fundamentalist and some mainstream churches, who are preaching healing, and/or 'deliverance' (with a need for repentance) from homosexuality.

The problem here is that the crucial message of Christianity actively and evangelically preaches inclusiveness to every person, with no distinctions.

How then can churches exclude lesbian, gay, or bisexual people from full membership, or ordination, if their lives exhibit sound citizenship, integrity, and love, together with a belief in Christ as their Saviour?

For if they are being excluded, then it is solely on a basis of (presumed) sexual practice being sinful, yet a declaration of sinless sexual practice is not required of others for church membership or ordination.

What does the Bible say/not say about Homosexuality?

Those churches which insist on the inerrancy of the Bible references to homosexuality do so in the face of much direct classical scholarship to the contrary, while at the same time they disregard, when expedient, many other biblical prohibitions. In essence it is not so much what the Bible says, but:

- the context (i.e. in what era the text was written and for what purposes) in which statements about homosexuality were made, and
- what was not said about homosexuality.

An explanation of the Bible texts on homosexuality can be found in the book by Bishop John Shelby Spong, Episcopalian Bishop of Newark, USA, called *Living in Sin? — a Bishop Rethinks Human Sexuality* (1988). Bishop Spong joins a growing number of theologians and biblical scholars who believe that many of the often quoted prohibitions on homosexual behaviour in the Bible have been mistranslated, or misquoted.

Many of these scholars are also saying that historical context is important, and that what may at one time have been a valuable rule of behaviour is not necessarily so today. For instance, at the time that Leviticus was written, the Israelites were a nomadic people, eking out a meagre existence in the desert. It may have been important for the survival of the tribe to ensure that procreation was maximised, but such a consideration surely does not apply today.

Bishop Spong and others also draw attention to a double-standard being applied by those who cite the Bible as their authority for condemning homosexual behaviour:

> *'The full story of Sodom (Gen.19, 1-11,), quoted so often to prove that the Bible condemns homosexuality [is] a strange text to use for such a purpose [for] it approves virgin daughters [being used] to satisfy sexual demands of an angry mob, suggests that incest is legitimate ... of women as [being a man's] property, and of gang rape [being acceptable] ... the real sin of Sodom was an unwillingness on the part of the men of the city to observe the laws of hospitality.'*
> (Spong, pp. 141-142)

Spong says that many literal statements of things forbidden or things endorsed, have long been disregarded even by those who hold the most literal views of the Biblical texts. For instance slavery, the abuse of women, certain food prohibitions, punishments such as stoning and other death penalties for infringements of ancient mythic codes, were taken for granted by Paul and earlier biblical writers. Today these revolt or amaze us in our more enlightened times. As our knowledge grew it was seen that these prohibitions suited the times, culture, and needs of the people then — these are not appropriate today.

In Spong's words:

> *'Those of us who have literalized the word of God, confining its creative power to a mould that accommodates only yesterday's wisdom, will not be able to adjust ... on the other hand, those of us who know that the dynamic Word of God cannot be bounded will be able to change, and grow, bringing to that Word our new ... perceptions of that eternal truth.'* (Spong p.164)

Some people (e.g. Barnett, 1976[2]) have argued that the biblical texts do not condemn (and may even endorse, in the case of David and Jonathon) loving, committed relationships between two men (or presumably two women), but rather condemn specific homosexual sins such as prostitution and rape. There is disagreement on this point, but it can certainly be said that all of the biblical references are to the use of sexual behaviour which is violent, rapist or exploitative, and not to homosexual orientation.

In a situation where there existed no conception of a range of natural sexual orientations, deviation from heterosexual behaviour would have seemed like a wilful rejection of the God-created 'natural order' of things and therefore sinful. It is also worthy of note that none of the alleged condemnations of homosexual behaviour is to be found in the Gospels, or in anything which Christ said.

What then of the 'Healing' of Homosexual Persons?

Some Christians, and some churches, are still confused

2 Barnett, Leo, *Homosexuality — Time to Tell the Truth*, 1975 Victor Gollancz Ltd, UK.

regarding sexual orientation, believing that a person always chooses their sexuality, and that therefore, because homosexual behaviour is 'sinful', homosexual men and lesbian women are all 'emotionally wounded, or unhappy', and must 'repent' to ensure success in being changed to (desirable?) heterosexuality. Celibacy (made possible by God) is a 'must' if change to heterosexuality cannot (after all) be effected.

It is possible that those orientated heterosexual people who have turned for whatever reason to homosexual behaviour, and are unhappy about this, can be assisted to revert to their basic heterosexuality with Christian love and support. Likewise it is possible any lesbians or gay men who are suffering from falsely imposed guilt and internalised homophobia can have their self-esteem rebuilt by loving Christian help that supports and accepts them as they are.

These fundamentalist groups are however insisting on, and still proclaiming, a 'blanket healing' for all. There is an obtuse non-acceptance of the fact that when a person's orientated sexuality is other than heterosexual, then this is but a natural variant which has no need to be, and indeed cannot be, 'changed'.

Moreover even should a person's sexuality behaviour have been perhaps established by other means at the age of two or three years, or maybe at fifty-two years, this does not imply it was a simple clear-cut 'decision', now amenable to 'cure' or 'persuasion'. It is certain to be a complex set of interwoven and subtle reactions built up over time. Furthermore, it is considered that none but the most skilled efforts to 'change' such behaviour which has become an integral part of the personality should be attempted, for such responses cannot be unlearned without trauma.

These groups also conveniently ignore that when a person's sexual identity and behaviour are not congruent with their orientated sexuality, the considerable stress induced by healing efforts may result in potentially disastrous consequences, including drug and alcohol abuse, depression, and suicide, or that these individuals may also be at increased risk of HIV infection.

Finally, when 'healing' fails, the defence is often: 'Sometimes it is God's will to "test" us (i.e. you) in a calling to celibacy and abstinence.'

[illegible] cut off from all deep, loving or affectionate same gender intimate relationships, homosexual people ordered to an imposed celibacy are literally condemned to a mental and emotional isolation and loneliness, not temporarily, but for life. Physically a person does not die from celibacy, but to ask it of those with stronger sexual needs is a cruelty few of the heterosexuals insisting on it would be prepared to personally accept.

There are three principal groups running 'conversion' programmes along these lines in New Zealand. These are the autonomous 'Exodus Ministries', 'Lion of Judah Ministries', and 'Rock of Life'. Many of those involved in similar groups overseas, including the former co-founders of 'Exodus' in the USA, have subsequently admitted their error.[3] They no longer believe that it is possible to change somebody's sexual orientation, or that the damaging personal costs for so many of those who attempt to change are justifiable.

There is ample documentation available and many wrote to me of lesbians and gay men who as a result of unthinking and thoughtless (if at times mistakenly loving) intervention have:

- tried marriage — to the resulting unhappiness of all involved, when this broke under the strain of the denial of their orientation

- could not leave such a marriage, genuinely caring for their spouse — but when the strains of coping grew too great went into closeted affairs, with the greater risk to all involved of STDs/HIV such behaviour brings

- through imposed guilt and homophobia been forced

3 Millen, Frederic, *The Advocate*, Los Angeles 4/12/90, Issue 565.

into lives of misery, tortured celibacy and loneliness committed suicide — I believe they did not die 'from being homosexual' but from the wrongly directed concern and bigotry, which did not allow them to be themselves.

Conclusion

Surely the real question is, 'Why should anyone try to change anyone else, or make them feel guilty about who they are?'

I believe that many sincere Christians are being bound by a homophobic and irrational fear based on misinformation and misunderstanding. There is certainly a fear of being asked to relax the boundaries of comfortable man-made rules and structures. Surely, whether as a minister, office-bearer or member of a church, a person is not called to serve its structures — but to follow Christ? No less is expected of Christian lesbians and gay men.

> *There is no fear in love, but perfect love casts out fear. For fear has to do with punishment, and he who fears is not perfected in love.'* (1 John 4:18)[4]

The church body is challenged, as was the Good Samaritan, to tenderly care for all others, to stand beside them, to offer them support — and love them as they are. This is both the simplest and the most difficult of all Christ's commandments.

I look for the day when lesbian, gay, and bisexual Christians will take their rightful place in the church fellowship, and in whatever denomination of their choice.

Jesus said: *'This is my commandment, that you love another, as I have loved you.'* (John 15:12)

---

4 Biblical texts from the *Revised Standard Version* (1971).

CHAPTER TWELVE

Helping Ourselves

Parents trying to understand a daughter [illegible] sexuality frequently feel shattered by th[illegible] ly emotional responses. These may be wide r[illegible] previously discussed, are often based on misinformation and/or an imposed guilt. Daughters and sons facing 'coming out' to themselves or others may experience similar reactions.

Being kind to oneself and recognising why these reactions occur helps, but it may be necessary to take positive action to overcome them. If, having done everything possible to help oneself over a reasonable length of time, painful reactions are still being experienced, then a professional counsellor or other well informed help is advised. To struggle on alone for too long is counter-productive. It is true that 'a trouble shared is a trouble halved'.

In experiencing painful emotions and facing up to them it will be found that new strengths and new hopes arise, and fresh challenges are born. There will also be a renewed loving tolerance of self and of others.

For some parents there may always be a small tinge of regret that a child is lesbian or gay. This is not non-acceptance, but rather a natural recognition that personally as a parent they might feel happier, and that life might perhaps be easier for their child, if she/he were heterosexual. However, when such regret recurs too often or becomes too preoccupying, then it is necessary to recognise that the causes for these emotions have not been completely dealt with.

The following self-help strategies are taken in part from pamphlets and other material supplied by the Northland Mental Health Trust and are used here by kind permission.

Bereavement and Grief

Grief affects not only those with a family member who has died. In a sense, for parents of lesbians and gay men there is a 'death' of cherished heterosexual expectations or beliefs. Hope of grandchildren, and more, seems to have been swept away.

Everyone needs to be aware that grief may be disguised. One may not specifically feel numbed, shocked, angry, resentful, sad or hopeless. Instead there may be feelings or a combination of feelings of either guilt, regret, anxiety, restlessness, irritability, or maybe of panic, tiredness, exhaustion and/or disorganisation.

Perhaps there may be physical discomfort — in the throat or stomach, headaches or shortness of breath, difficulty in eating or sleeping, or lack of concentration. There may be feelings of confusion, fear, or disbelief. There may be an inability to accept what has been said.

These feelings may be intense, appear in several combinations, or vary from person to person.

Mourning has recognised stages. These may be felt by anyone in a variety of grief situations. Frequently grief over a child being lesbian or gay goes through much the same process.

There are no hard and fast limits on how long a stage may take, but sometimes people 'get stuck' on a stage and counselling may be helpful to move on towards healthy healing and acceptance.

The grief process may include:

- Denial — emotional release — pain — bargaining with God.
- Anger — guilt — blaming — aloneness — panic — depression.
- Acceptance — hope — living with the loss; until ... life looks good again.

It helps to recognise that there will be triggers, or reminders that temporarily set back progress. These will become further spaced with time.

It is known that some men find it harder to openly grieve, being conditioned from childhood not to cry easily. Encouragement may be needed to allow fathers to express their feelings in more constructive ways than by burying them in such coping strategies as over-work, over-use of alcohol or denial. (Mothers or others may bury their grief in these ways, too.)

Other family members may also be grieving. Each will deal with their grief in different ways. Everyone needs to be encouraged to help each other and maintain the other aspects of the family relationships.

If a daughter or son actually dies, it needs to be recognised that their long-term partner is the principal mourner. Her/his wishes, hard though this may be for some parents, are to be respected. A sensitive partner will consider parental wishes in funeral arrangements. The last wishes of the deceased, as far as is practical, should be adhered to.

Anger

Anger is a natural emotion. It is a normal reaction to loss, and an essential part of grief. Anger can be triggered by many things, including insults, injustice, frustration or prejudicial beliefs. Taking anger out on other people does not help anyone.

The body signals of anger are the heart beating faster; altered breathing patterns; muscles tensing in the chest, neck, face, arms and legs; stomach, head, neck or backache; sweating or feeling cold and clammy.

In behaviour there may be altered sleeping or eating patterns; meanness and finding blame towards others; depression, withdrawal, or quietness; punishing of others by 'not speaking'; being sarcastic or laughing it off; having difficulty in following through on commitments.

To deal with anger it is NOT helpful to deny the anger; blame others; try to 'hit' back; take drugs such as nicotine, alcohol, cannabis, headache tablets, or tranquillisers.

Temporary relief may be found by walking away from the immediate conflict taking 'time out', speaking out of feelings; telling someone else about it. Physical activity such as working, jogging, or gardening helps to work off the stress that can build up.

How anger is dealt with is important. The more a person is aware of their being angry, the less chance there is of losing control.

Anger indicates that a situation needs changing, which sometimes means in the person experiencing the anger — not only in others! It needs to be asked what needs changing and is this realistically likely to change? Maybe it is one's own expectations or idealism that is the problem? Or is it the situation or the relationship?

Finally, only action will dissolve anger. Question the basis of beliefs, get good information and personal support while the situation is being worked out.

Conflict

People may experience more internal conflict than anger. Conflict can be subtle, unrecognised, passively aggressive or openly destructive.

Parents may have a whole range of inner conflicting emotions about lesbianism and gayness. So too may their daughters and sons, having been raised with heterosexual expectations.

Everyone in the situation may rush into expressing their own needs. Open conflict may result, which can damage relationships, maybe for years. The first thing to remember is that conflict is common and arises easily where there are differences of opinion. Also, remember that living with conflict can be tiring and upsetting; giving in may not help, and both sides may be partly right on some issues.

Conflict can be productive, but it needs to be handled carefully. What can be done?

- Work out how it is affecting oneself and others.
- Try to work out the real causes.
- Try to discuss the problem.
- Try to understand the other person's feelings.

It helps to listen to other points of view and give others the benefit of the doubt. Most importantly, be prepared to make sure your information is true — check it out.

Conflicts may wreck relationships if not dealt with and speedily resolved. Certainly at times everyone needs advice, but parents with the best of intentions who wish to save their children grief may have to 'let them go'. This is not easy. If daughters and sons can rely on parental support and leave home with firmly grounded good self-esteem, the parents' job will have been well done.

Self-Esteem

A universal problem for most people is self-esteem — how good one feels about oneself It depends on how one's strengths are valued, as well as a willingness to make changes. Like many adults, parents may carry and react to 'messages' from the past, and tend to pass these on to daughters and sons. In general, as an adult, one cannot give to children what one has never learned — and children cannot be, or react to, other than what they have absorbed or been taught. It is a self-perpetuating circle — but this can be broken.

It is acknowledged there may be strong reasons for a parent feeling guilty and thinking they have 'caused' a daughter or son to be homosexual. A daughter or son may also feel strongly that there are reasons to blame parents. It is the past actions or events which need to be dealt with, for only then can homosexuality be seen clearly as the separate issue it is.

In general, many of our actions are but a response to past experiences. These may have produced distorted needs, lack of insight, or lack of knowledge. In this there can be no direct blame towards ourselves or others.

When these distinctions are understood, the healing for any past hurts against others is by forgiveness of others and/or of self. Nobody has perfect parents, and nobody has perfect kids! At some point in life it is necessary to accept being an adult by becoming responsible for personal actions. For the sake of all concerned, be very sure that feelings of 'imposed' guilt, insecurity, or denial of a child's (or one's own) orientation are not taken out upon them (or upon one's parents or partner).

As I learnt by throwing off my state of imposed guilt, as described earlier, we can all be enabled to reject feelings from past events which allow us to remain 'victimised'. In reality no situation can make us a victim if we get good information, support for ourselves, and utilise our own power.

In reacting emotionally to situations which are seen to affect social status, a person can feel very threatened, tending to look for someone or something to blame. This relates to imposed shame; 'blaming' occurs because we have been taught that homosexuality is 'wrong' — this is homophobia! Often it may not be recognised that this 'blaming' has become rooted in lowered self-esteem and by the fear such insecurity induces.

Self-image is affected by what it is felt others think of one; by the love of friends, which gives feelings of self-worth; or by any frequent criticism and argument which produces feelings of isolation and depression — this includes self-criticism, self put-downs, feelings of not fitting in, and the fear of being 'different'.

It does not help to:

- Withdraw — hiding away from oneself or others
- Be aggressive — fighting with others or constantly arguing
- Clown — by making a fool of oneself
- Deny what is happening — pretending the situation will go away
- Deaden the pain — by using drugs or alcohol
- Conform — doing what others say to keep the peace, or because it is not known how to explain.

It can help to:

- Get good information and support
- Set new goals that can be reached
- Learn to say 'No'; and to look after one's health
- Give encouragement, a gift, a smile, or a compliment to someone else
- Accept that it is okay to be oneself, and okay to love oneself
- Learn to accept compliments, and to stand tall.

Loneliness (Mainly for Daughters and Sons)

This often results from shyness or fear. Whether you are younger or older, it is best to begin in small ways to break this down. Start by talking to one person, maybe someone at the local lesbian or gay phone switchboard (many of which services are toll-free). From this it will become comfortable to meet someone from a support group face-to-face. When more confident, consider joining a 'newcomers' group. Most larger and well-established lesbian and gay support organisations offer such sessions, as well as sessions for those in the process of coming out.

There should be no pressure to do anything uncomfortable. If you are not in fact lesbian or gay, going to a group will not 'make' you what you are not, but it may settle any fears. if you are lesbian or gay, there will be accepting friendship, with supportive information available both for you personally and for when a decision is made to come out to parents. Frequently such support groups will have other parent contacts in your area from whom your parents can receive support.

Be assertive about going at a comfortable pace, and doing what feels right personally. Say 'not yet' or 'no' when something feels wrong. Everybody has their own timing and way of doing things. Relax. Remember, it is definitely okay to be yourself and to be non-heterosexual.

Jealousy in Relationships

Jealousy is a miserable emotion which everyone experiences at some time or another — particularly in close relationships with others. Where there is poor self-esteem, this can contribute to personal insecurity, allowing jealousy to flourish more easily.

When it seems everyone else is happier, more loved, more liked, more talented, or more attractive — dwelling on this only serves to make oneself unhappy. Sometimes out of this misery a person will then set out to make loved ones jealous. Working out jealousy on others may be a form of avoiding conflict or needed discussion, evading the need to be assertive and calmly say what needs to be aired. Then, having exploded angrily from pent-up feelings and provoked a row, the other person is blamed for not being the reasonable one! Making up may be sweet, but only until the next time, or until, fed up, they walk out — frequently to someone else.

Longer Relationship Survival

Homosexual daughters or sons, with few or no available role models, may expect a relationship to follow those of the heterosexual people around them and their parents may also expect this. Homosexual relationships do not repeat the pattern of heterosexual marriages; instead, it is being found, they have their own patterns, stages and styles of continuance.

Once it was acceptable to play the field and live up to the 'free love' image. Today, as my questionnaire responses showed, many lesbians and gay men are hoping for long-term romance and steady relationships.

No partnership works without compromise, adjustment and well worked out rules for emotional trust, which are applicable to both people involved. The affection which well-adjusted lesbians or gay men feel for their partner is comparable in terms of gentleness, admiration, pride and self-denial to that of a man and a woman in the best of loving heterosexual relationships. All these qualities are reinforced by sexual attraction or drive, whatever one's sexual orientation. Many gay men have tenderly nursed lovers or other friends through illness or in some cases the trauma of dying with AIDS.

Sexual availability or compatibility alone is not often the foundation of a long-term romance. It is the acceptance of differences, the ability to allow others their 'space', the sharing of toothpaste, of sunsets or sunrises, and of the chores, which builds long-term 'togetherness'. All relationships need constant review and input from both partners to remain exciting and successful. Nothing kills romance quicker than taking the other person too much for granted!

When relationships become difficult or things go wrong, it is so much easier to walk away or blame everyone else. When one has not yet achieved or recognised the need for self-insight, the problems in any relationships — be they parental, with partners, or friends — can be overwhelming.

Sometimes other worries in life are affecting one at the same time, and depression[1] may set in and undermine one's ability to cope.

In Conclusion for Everyone

Overcoming upsetting emotional responses involves making changes. Relief will only be permanent where some of one's own beliefs, ideas and behaviours are changed, with a willingness to take a look at how one perceives things and to meet others at least half-way.

Ultimately, of course, it is only oneself — whether as a parent, or as a daughter or son — who is responsible for personal thoughts and actions towards oneself and other people.

It may be necessary to see a counsellor. In seeking professional counselling it is advisable to seek advice from an accredited agency such as the NZ AIDS Foundation, Lesbian Lines, Gay Switchboards, Lifeline, mental health or youth support services. These will recommend trained therapists to suit particular needs.

1 Please note: If depression persists or is severe, it is necessary to seek help from a doctor or a professional counsellor.

CHAPTER THIRTEEN

Legal Issues

Throughout the history of civilisation there have been lengthy periods when gay people have been accepted in society, and periods when they have been subjugated to varying degrees of oppression, sometimes to the point of mass murder, as in Hitler's Germany where very many homosexual men, marked by the pink triangle, were killed in the death camps.

Laws against homosexual behaviour and persecution have meant that gay men have been driven into meeting under clandestine conditions, into marriage as a protective front, leading 'double lives', to the debilitation of their whole well-being. They have also been driven to suicide. That a code of morality was enforced on them by others who frequently led less than chaste sexual lives was conveniently ignored.

It is fair to say, however, that as society has become more highly educated, with knowledge and learning vastly increasing, society has become less dependent upon primitive fear and superstition. Therefore the demand that gay people conceal their sexual orientation has been steadily decreasing.

There are several legal issues of which lesbian, gay and bisexual daughters and sons need to be aware. Parents of younger daughters and sons also need to be aware of these and offer guidance when appropriate. Foresight can save much anguish later.

Relationship Status

The right to marry is taken for granted by most parents, but may not be available to our children. Legal rights vary worldwide according to the constitution, laws and the decisions by judges in each country. Marriage rights may or may not exist, there may be a legal equivalent to marriage or a relationship record that has no legal effect. The differences can affect the legal rights of adults and children.

Reasons for marriage equality include (see further australianmarriageequality.com):

- Legal security, such as inheritance, parental rights and contact rights in an emergency.
- Public commitment. An existing relationship may be strengthened or it is simply romantic for a couple who are in love.
- Social and cultural recognition.
- Religious freedom is enhanced.
- Children may benefit from all of the above.

In addition:

> *'Allowing same-sex couples to marry will admit many more couples who seek to uphold the core values of marriage and are enthusiastic for the institution. It will send out the message that marriage is defined by love and respect not prejudice and discrimination. It will also prompt opposite-sex couples to re-value wedlock as an institution in which the over-arching values are love, devotion, and not least, social inclusion. Allowing same-sex couples to marry will show that marriage is relevant and resilient enough to embrace changing social attitudes in the same way it did last century when married women were given legal equality and interracial marriages were allowed.'* (australianmarriageequality.com).

Contracts and Wills

There may be no law in your country which gives 'as of right' protection to either party in a lesbian or gay relationship in relation to property or financial matters. However it may be legal to draw up personal agreements, which would then be upheld in a court of law. These should detail:

- Financial particulars as to property ownership and division of related debt-servicing responsibilities.
- What is to happen upon any later dissolution of the partnership.
- Provisions for a legal contract to enable someone trustworthy to handle personal business, should either partner become mentally or physically incapacitated. The full meaning of the contract and its responsibilities can be clearly explained by a legal advisor.

In addition, a will for each person should be drawn up to decide what happens to their assets if they die. Otherwise their relatives may control the estate, not the partner.

A will should:

- Cover all aspects of shared land, dwellings, stockmarket shares, insurance, furnishings or expensive items such as cars, jewellery, etc.
- Clarify bequests to a partner and to family members; and cover any aspects of funeral wishes desired.
- Appoint a legal guardianship for any children.
- Make appointment of a trustworthy person to be the executor of the estate.

A will can be updated as often as needed at little cost. It is vital to revise it every few years, or immediately there is a significant change in personal circumstances.

Artificial Insemination and Adoption

Lesbian couples seeking private donor artificial insemination to induce pregnancy (in the absence of a government program) need to be very clear on certain issues:

- What will the donor father's position be in relation to the child?
- What access to the child will he have/not have?
- What is to happen to the child where a lesbian couple seeking custody later separate, or if one or both should die.
- What contributions should be made, and by whom, for the child's financial and other support?
- The donor's health needs clarification, particularly regarding STDs and/or HIV/AIDS.

A contract is essential. Discussions, before the donation is accomplished, should be recorded, as people's memories are fallible and informal discussions are not always legally enforceable.

Should a gay man wish to be a donor for artificial insemination he needs to be aware that:

- Even if an agreement as to the financial support for a child is waived, this can be changed if any subsequent application by the mother to the court for support is upheld.

- Child support may be enforceable until the child is an adult, depending on the law in your country.

- Even if the father is not recorded on the birth certificate, paternity may at some point be decided by the court, as the child's welfare is paramount. DNA testing is taken as conclusive, there being only a one in several million chance of error in most tests.

- Should the donor not be truthful about HIV/AIDS, Hepatitis B, or other sexually transmitted diseases, he may later be liable for support if the child is born infected.

Similar issues of access, custody and financial liability arise in cases of adoption. A contract is essential in the absence of a government program. Last, for all concerned, it is unwise to enter into any contract with a person, either female or male, who uses illegal drugs.

Harassment, Rape or Blackmail

There may or may not be specific laws that protect people in your country from discrimination on the grounds of their sexual orientation. If not, some general protection may still be granted by the law. For instance:

- If subjected to threatening behaviour or minor assault.

- If subjected to rape (whether male or female) or any major assault.

- If regular threatening abuse by telephone is received, This may come under the telecommunications law.

- If subjected to blackmail.

International Legal Status

It may not be fully realised by younger people travelling abroad for the first time that the tolerant legal situation at home may be very different in other countries. It is essential to be aware of the laws on homosexual activity in other places before arriving there. Some countries have laws specifically against lesbians, as well as against gay men.

In federal countries like the USA or Australia, the laws frequently vary from state to state. Developed countries all have AIDS organisations which may be able to give advice on the local situation if contacted.

The International Lesbian, Gay, Bisexual, Trans and Intersex Association maintains a worldwide inventory of discrimination and liberation for lesbians and gay men. This documents every country where legal status is known, including marriage rights (see ilga.org).

CHAPTER FOURTEEN

Sexuality Education

Public attitudes shape oppression. It is reinforced and carried by word of mouth, through literature, the radio, and by the visual influence of theatre, films, video and television. We are affected deeply, if unconsciously, by the media which surround us. The messages we receive begin in earliest childhood, and are reinforced by the attitudes of the adults around us. The whispers and innuendos grow. By late primary school age we are calling others 'sissy', 'poofy,", or 'lessy' without any real understanding. As we grow older the vindictiveness and victimisation deepens. We fear anyone who is 'different' in our own adolescent (and later adult) insecurity. As adults we may fail to re-think these attitudes or question the information absorbed.

The paramount concern is that many homosexual teenagers, particularly those not living in or near the major cities, have at present few avenues through which to discover their sexuality, unlike their heterosexual siblings. I now understand and believe that parents and schools urgently need to be more accountable to these young people. We need to provide them with appropriate information and support, and to encourage the responsible people within the lesbian and gay community and other organisations who are struggling to provide this service.

What Schools Can, and Many Don't, Do

The most important resource towards understanding homosexuality and bisexuality is education. Many people have feared 'contagion, promiscuity, disease, and recruitment' if inclusive sexuality education is promoted. The reality is the opposite. There will be lives saved, a strengthening of mental health, and less promiscuity if better acceptance is achieved through professionally promoted and delivered education.

There is public paranoia that education of the young on inclusive sexualities by freedom of information will become a matter of 'conversion'. This is not so, it is rather a matter of 'self discovery' for those who are — and those who are not — lesbian, gay or bisexual. People who assert that children must be 'protected' from knowledge of such sexualities are not being realistic. Further, the implication is that any knowledge of homosexuality or bisexuality would make it seem so attractive that everyone who is heterosexual would immediately want to change their sexuality!

Schools obviously are not insulated from outside influences, but have the same beliefs, attitudes, and opinions as the rest of the population. Many children 'learn' about lesbianism and gayness — but what they 'learn' is likely to be myth, misinformation and prejudice, for these flourish where no deliberate action is being taken to inform.

Exclusion in teaching will not 'protect' our children or stop them from coming into contact with other sexualities, rather it will ensure that they will hold unbalanced and prejudicial views. Too many of our children are suffering (and killing themselves) from the pressures, the teasing, the physical abuse and mental torture inflicted on them (albeit unthinkingly) by peers, and in some cases by those whose duty it is to protect them at home, at school and in society.

Young people, when first aware of their own lesbianism, gayness or bisexuality, are greeted by a dreadful 'conspiracy of silence'. Feeling desperately isolated, fearing they are mad or crazy, they rarely have anyone in whom to confide. They seek information from outdated literature, secretly look up words in dictionaries whose definitions may well be from the out-dated theories of the 1960s. If they are from church-going families they may hear homosexuality is 'sinful and abominable' — adding self-loathing and guilt to the burden of being 'different'.

Within the school environment, the person allocated to fill the 'listening role' is the school counsellor. Even if sympathetic, they may have no real help to give, or be under instruction not to 'encourage such lifestyles'. If uninformed, they may direct these young people to inappropriate psychological counselling — with or without parental consent. A young person may fear their confidence will not be honoured and not take the risk of approaching an adult for help. It may be impossible for them to get private access to a phone to contact an agency such as Youth Help.

Ann-Marie Stapp wrote her recent master's thesis on the lives of young lesbians in New Zealand.[1] She observed:

> *'In schools there is a high level of mental abuse, both direct and indirect. The harassment, verbal abuse, the physical abuse and even the silence about lesbian [and gay] lives, causes considerable mental and emotional pain.'*

Parents in their questionnaire responses also mentioned these issues. They said:

'We need education in schools on homosexuality, for pupils, teachers and counsellors. School can be a nightmare for children when they are experiencing different attractions from those expected. Others are "guessed" to be lesbian or gay and suffer real persecution, from pupils and staff alike.' (Parent)

'My son had mud, faeces and urine dumped on him in the night and was rolled in it. It got so he couldn't sleep, his work suffered, and he became suicidally depressed. He was "accidentally" pushed down a bank, and his forearm was hairline fractured. Boarding schools need to teach anti-discrimination, be more aware and tighten supervision.' (Father)

1 Stapp, Ann-Marie, 'Coming Out as a Young Lesbian' 1990 Thesis, Victoria University of Wellington.

'My son at only eight years was sprayed with perfume on the school bus by older kids and called names. Later in high school he was taunted as being an AIDS carrier, he was distraught at times.' (Mother)

These statements were corroborated by a New Zealand Department of Health report, *Adolescent Sexuality* (1990), which said:

> *'Society in general holds the attitude that anyone who is not heterosexual is abnormal, and being abnormal is dirty and disgusting. Parents put extensive energy into encouraging their sons to be macho, that is not show any feminine traits, and their daughters to be acceptably feminine. Sexuality education needs to incorporate a sense of understanding feelings, including sexual feelings, of themselves and others ... the universal value of not exploiting or hurting one another... it needs to target the reduction of fear of sex-related activities ...'*

The report recommended that schools:

- establish programmes which take into account the background and circumstances of all young people, including those with different abilities and (sexual) orientations

- make available to young people and families information as to their individual rights, the resources for advocacy available to them, and how these resources may be accessed

- establish appropriate teacher models in every school for the sexuality component within a comprehensive school health programme

- make available to teachers skilled facilitators for school-based training in sexuality education include education about sexually transmitted diseases in sexuality education

and that

- single-sex schools be encouraged to introduce comprehensive health and sexuality programmes.

In this age of reduction in government spending for specialized programmes in education, we will have to lobby for these strategies to be implemented, whether as parents, educators, or members of the caring general public.

It is necessary to ensure programmes in schools that will:

- remove the fears about homosexuality which lead to anger, violence, and derision

- counteract sexist conditioning, by providing information about gender differentiation and the fallacies of stereotyping

- provide lesbian, gay, bisexual and transsexual students with positive information about themselves

- ensure training of all school staff in comprehensive sexuality issues, and suicide prevention.

In *The Healthy Sexual Development of Gay and Lesbian Adolescents* (1990),[2] Gary Remafedi says:

> *'In my vision of ideal sexual development, all young people will participate in comprehensive sexuality education in their schools, which will demystify sexuality including homo-*

2 Remafedi, Gary (May-June 1990) *The Healthy Development of Gay and Lesbian Adolescents*, SIERCUS Report.

sexuality, normalize "sex talk", and help boys overcome the need to sexualize everything in their lives. Such education will raise self esteem and will empower all youth, regardless of their sexual orientation.'

Conclusion

Past generations have tended to accept a double-standard of 'discreet adventures' for boys and 'innocence as its own protection' for girls — which often it was not. Heterosexuality was compulsory. Girls were often warned about, or quickly perceived men to be 'dangerous creatures with unruly passions'. If they as girls 'disgraced the family' — the disgrace was not specified — they could expect to be sent away from home. Ignorance was rife. It is surprising women had enough courage to marry and have children at all! Some held on to their individuality and did not marry, but at great personal social cost.

Regrettably these attitudes and double standards are still being upheld, even more unrealistically in this age of television, videos, advertising media and fresh insights. Today young people are experimenting sexually earlier. They are prey to many more social dangers than my own generation. And while some schools — and groups such as the New Zealand Family Planning Association — have made progress in this field, all the young people of this country still urgently need a nationally co-ordinated, professionally delivered, comprehensively inclusive sexuality educational programme which promotes care of self and others.

I believe action to ensure this is the pressing responsibility of government and of us all.

CHAPTER FIFTEEN

For Parents, and For Daughters and Sons

The last question on my questionnaire asked: 'Have you any thoughts you would like to share with other parents or daughters and sons?' All respondents wrote from the heart here, many very graphically and at great length. A selection is given from those received.

Responses from Parents

'The important thing is to never stop loving your child. When they come out they need your love and acceptance more than ever. Also, don't be too hard on yourself as a parent, give yourself time to come to terms with the news.'

'Don't take it for granted that they know you love and understand. They are vulnerable and need your reassurance. It's easy for them to misinterpret your remarks, because they are extra sensitive to criticism. Their self-esteem needs boosting because they are aware of much disapproval. If you are worried find a well informed counsellor.'

'Having seen the depression my son had, and now realising the trauma he experienced over a long period, I feel we as parents should have shown more support by discussing the possibility of homosexuality. He suffered years of anguish before accepting himself, and being accepted by us.'

'My best advice came from a counsellor, he said it is most important to think and say not "my gay son", but "my son, who is gay". This puts the stress in the right place. I have retained the love of my son with this attitude, and have gained a wonderful friend.'

'Come to terms with the fact that your child is a special unique person, who is entitled to live without hiding his true self, and always living a lie. Don't take away your love and support — that is the most important thing of all.'

'I never thought I'd say this, but it's hard when their long-term relationship breaks up. I'm as sad as they are. We love his partner, he became our other son. It's no different to any other child's relationship splitting up.'

'Six years down the track it all seems insignificant. It could have been much worse — like an incurable disease. He is still the same loving person. Coming to grips with the (thought of a) partner was a worry — but proved needless.'

'I found this in a book: "I believe we're never given anything in life which we are unable to withstand. From the quiet settling of pain comes hope and gratitude for the rewards that come from that newly realised strength." That's what parenthood is really, isn't it? — painful at times but rewarding.'

'My initial reactions have changed. I have been totally honest about my own feelings good or bad, and we have talked through these — which helped me to accept. They have not stayed with me yet, and I still find the physical attraction between them difficult. I realise we have to be realistic. I have told them (they are welcome): home is home. I have tried to make his partner, whom I like very much, feel at ease.'

'Providing a stable, loving, accepting family, and a "safe" place for our son is paramount. He is a high school seventh former, and we also see that it should make no difference to his ambitions, values or responsibilities in life. We allow him to have his friends home (both straight and gay), our only house rule is "good taste" in any more overt behaviour, especially around his grandparents and our friends.'

'Please don't turn your back, encourage them to talk to you. Let them know it's no fault of their own.'

'Welcome their friends, give them a place to meet, keep the lines of communication open.'

'It's not always understood that the family are doing their best to be supportive. My daughter has been very changeable in her attitudes and this is disconcerting. Her husband initially was suicidal and we had to support him, as he has no other family here.'

'Be supportive of their relationships. When these get broken it can be very disturbing for them, they need someone to listen.'

'Our worst time was before she came out, as she had rejected us, especially the male members of our family, and we didn't know or understand why. I dodged the word "lesbian" for several years. She has gradually come back to us, and her relationship now is very stable and happy.'

'His sexuality has nothing to do with his value as a human being.'

Many parents of both daughters and sons made similar comments.

Responses from Sons

'I only wish society was more accepting, and people could be more open without harassment.'

'In the past I've met so many gay men that are grieving for their parents' love and acceptance that is denied them because of their homosexuality. This is a great tragedy as everyone suffers.'

'Parents should not presume their child is straight. They should support them, not influence or pressure them.'

'Coming out is a statement of growing self-esteem, and parents should help nurture it. Sons and daughters should build on the love and trust of parents and not be defensive or aggressive, and explain to their parents that acceptance takes time.'

'I'm not wanted to baby-sit my nieces and nephews any more — that hurts. I am going to live my own life, and not by the way others want me to. They see my way of life as wrong — I don't.'

'Acceptance of oneself is the ultimate key. The more accepting we are of ourselves the more this will be reflected outwardly in our reality. People pick on weakness, they will not pick on strength. We are not "victims" — this takes away our self-empowerment. If we focus on oppression we will be oppressed. We can choose to be positive or negative.'

'I think that I expected too much of my parents. I had struggled with my sexuality for years. Eventually I accepted it and came out. I felt upset when I realised that they would need some time adjusting to the news.'

'My greatest fear was my father's reaction. If I had known my family would accept me as well as they have, I would have told them sooner.'

'Without the nurturing love of my family I would have found coming out most difficult. Now I have a gay family as well. I feel most fortunate.'

'I know friends that are hurting inside, wanting to tell their parents, and are breaking away from them, because they can't tell them.'

'I feel if I could tell my parent's I am gay, I would be able to get on with them better. It is hard for me at family functions to not have my partner there, I feel a bit left out.'

'Try to reach the point where you are no longer afraid of your sexuality. To be open and unafraid of who you are does two things. It makes you free and it liberates others. It is not something you can do overnight. It takes time, a lot of small steps and a little bit of courage, but you can do it! To parents — you may be your child's last refuge, don't destroy it for them.'

'I'm not too thrilled about what some heterosexual people do in bed either.'

'Many religious parents don't appreciate they brought their child up to be honest, then reject him for being truthful and not wanting to live a lie. They talk about God loving everyone and don't love their own child.'

'My parents found out I was gay by reading my diary! This was traumatic in itself, but I was locked out of the house for a weekend and they didn't speak to me for quite a while.

We are still having arguments eighteen months later. I'm still trying to prove my worth and I think there is a slow shifting in perspective. I took a (male) partner to the school ball and those who know me there don't mind.'

'We are just as good as straight kids — we just want to be loved. Love — is understanding.'

'Variation is the peak of God's creativity.'

Responses from Daughters

'The best thing my parents did was to keep an open mind. They realised how hard it was for us to tell them and respected this. [Family has more than one lesbian or gay child]. They also showed interest by learning more, by talking, reading, etc. That was very important for getting rid of preconceptions and gaining understanding.'

'Don't reject your child. They usually don't suddenly become this monstrosity from your deepest nightmare — they need your love and support.'

'We are many things, we all look different. Encourage us to be proud of who we are. Silence can be as condemning and homophobic as blatant negative statements. Work through your own assumptions and biases, but don't put us in little categorised boxes.'

'If it was safer for us to come out of the closet I believe that problems with alcohol and drug addictions within our group would drop dramatically. Please love us as we are.'

'The hardest part of being gay is telling your parents. Most of us live with the stigma of trying to please them. So when they don't accept it, or can't, it's emotionally very hard on us.'

'If we felt accepted as teenagers, lesbianism and gayness would be seen as positive. We would not hurt others, or rush into unsuitable relationships.'

'My parents gave us house-warming presents of a toaster and a dinner-set, to welcome my lover into our family I'm delighted with them. I think they deserve celebrating.'

'I feel their prejudice has caused them more problems than I have. I'm sad for them because they're missing out on sharing my life. I'm also sad because I can tolerate so little of their company at present, because they have very little regard for how I feel.'

There were many more comments. It was, of course, impossible to quote everyone. You all contributed to the contents and overall emphasis of this book. You are all represented directly or indirectly in it somewhere.

Responses from Family Members

Family members provide the last word. After all, they see both sides of the parent-child relationship. As close onlookers, they often have to support those involved and even referee at times.

'To other family members accept the fact and continue to love each other. Life is too short to waste precious family love and sharing.' (Brother)

'I have several lesbian and gay friends (my sister is one of my best friends), they are the warmest, caring, sharing people I know. It takes enormous courage to come out. So it you suspect a family member is gay, maybe you could ask and help them.' (Sister)

'I've been a go-between for ten years trying to get my parents to lighten up.' (Sister)

'I believe that if anyone degrades gay people in any way, others should speak out against this — it's comparable to racism. It takes guts to do this, but if it's done in the right manner it can change people's opinions.' (Sister)

'My sister made a conscious choice to be a lesbian. She had a natural preference to be in the social and intimate company of women. This is where she feels most comfortable and happy. After all happiness is everyone's ultimate goal, and I want her to be happy.' (Sister)

What more can I add? Every parent, son, daughter, or other family member has said it all eloquently~ at times painfully, and so lovingly. I believe that the families who have opened themselves to fresh insights, while remaining united by love, have gained enormous benefits in deeper commitment to each other. Several, like ourselves, found new understanding, which brought unexpected joys and strengths. I hope this will be the reality for your family.

CHAPTER SIXTEEN

Beyond 'Acceptance' — Pro-action

'We hold these truths to be sacred and undeniable; that all men [and women] are created equal and independent, that from equal creation they derive rights inherent and inalienable, among which are the preservation of life, and liberty, and the pursuit of happiness.'
from the original draft for the American Declaration of Independence by President Thomas Jefferson.

It is evident that the majority of lesbians and gay men are, against considerable odds, well balanced, caring, and good citizens. I believe that if society in general would allow them to come out without fear or trauma to be themselves, they would all be enabled to have good self-esteem and better mental health.

In the final analysis, 'cause' of homosexuality is not an issue — apart from the need to be sure that the basis of our beliefs is correct and well informed. People are as they are, their orientated sexuality cannot be changed. Sexual behaviour and sexual identity are different issues.

It is my strongest hope that having read this book you have been empowered to reach this point of understanding. Now I encourage you to go beyond mere knowledge. Listed here are some of the caring measures you might take to actively help to end prejudice and discrimination:

- Provide your school Board of Trustees with information and request inclusive sexuality education; request firm policies against lesbian/gay harassment; request encouragement of lesbian/gay staff to be visible as good role models.

- Provide information for school library, counsellors' rooms and community noticeboards.

- Promote the inclusion of lesbian and gay literature, both fiction and non-fiction, in school libraries and the local public libraries.

- Lobby the government for support and finance for education in the prevention of suicide, HIV/AIDS and STDs; and for human rights legislation (or its enforcement) to protect people from discrimination on the grounds of their sexual orientation, or HIV status.

- Whenever appropriate, inform your other family, friends and neighbours on what being lesbian/gay really is; speak against prejudice.

- Write to the local media when it is homophobic or presents false information.

- Welcome your daughter's, son's, or relative's friends or partner into your home.

- When a long-term partner stays, provide shared bedroom accommodation. Invite their partner to family occasions; give equal value presents for Christmas and birthdays; and give a house-warming gift.

- Encourage the development of gay community ventures in health and support services, but do not try to step in and manage them.

- Assist your local AIDS Support, and local lesbian/gay groups when applicable; consider offering your name as a phone contact for 'new' parents support; or maybe join, or start a parent support group in your area.

In Conclusion

To lay aside prejudice and embrace new ideas is a challenge to us, whether we are younger or older. It can be a great shock to discover (and it is sometimes hard to acknowledge) that for much of our life we have subscribed to or perpetrated (even by default) misinformation about sexuality without looking more deeply into the issues involved.

Not only may parents have to acknowledge this and the hurts they may have, albeit unwittingly, caused to their children — but so too their daughters and sons may need to acknowledge the effort and personal re-assessment undertaken by their parents to achieve understanding.

I am particularly conscious that nothing I have written can be of any comfort to those whose loved ones have died, whether from AIDS or from suicide. I can only encourage you to join the lobby for inclusive sexuality education; to support those who work to end discrimination and educate on the prevention of the spread of HIV/AIDS; or to assist those services which aid and care for the ill or dying which need our help. I do not forget that many of you have been involved to the point of exhaustion. I acknowledge and honour your efforts.

If, for any reason, when someone has died (or attempted to die) we feel angry at them, or regretful we were not more understanding or helpful towards them, it is necessary to recognise that there is no need to blame them or ourselves for being human — we all make errors. Any 'crime' is in not forgiving, in punishing them/ ourselves, or in not trying to put right any mistakes if this is still possible. In the latter we may not always be successful, but we will be strengthened by the effort.

I find it comforting, maybe you will also, to think of a person's spent life force as being regenerated through the outward love we go on expressing to each other, whether in our birth family, in our lesbian or gay family, or toward the world. Together, we are able to forge a new experience and a deeper perception. This strengthens us as we go onward, participating fully in life, as they would surely want us to do — with courage.

As humankind, we are multi-dimensional beings, having a wholeness that comprises mental, emotional, sexual and physical inherent talents — each of which are interwoven with a spiritual capacity. Maori have accepted this in their integrated concept of aroha (love), wairua (spirit), reo (language) and whanau (family). This total spiritual essence, which may have but does not necessarily include a religious observance, demands from us all a balanced perspective.

It is my observation that no belief, talent, ability or interest followed exclusively or obsessively will lead to our fulfilment. Rather it will lead eventually to a state of great stress and imbalance. Our position then easily becomes delusional, moving inexorably across the dividing line from good intent to ill result. This is an individual and heavy responsibility. It may mean that a belief or action of itself can become so necessary to us personally that by insisting on holding to it we become willing (even if by default or indirectly) to cause another person to despair.

Fortunately we each have a measure of personal power. We can for instance choose to give to others or to rob them. We can help assert their rights or try to deny them those rights. Likewise we may use our sexuality to our well-being and that of others, or to abuse them and ourselves.

It is worth reflecting that even in the first century AD Epictetus observed:

> *'People are not disturbed by things, but by the views which they take of them.'*

Regretfully I am no saint. At times I find my anger or disappointment will not change the views of others! However, I do basically trust and work towards the balance of love, reason, justice and humanity which, together with good information, will give me the key to solve misunderstandings, disagreements or problems.

It has been my privilege, and it has helped me enormously, to share my thoughts and our personal journey of information-finding with you. I sincerely believe you will now be able to recognise, as Ron and I have been enabled to do, that:

- A person's orientated sexuality, be it heterosexual, bisexual, or homosexual, is indivisible from their total person.

- Overall it is the integrity, genuine love and caring exhibited in a person's life which matters.

- We all need unconditional love and encouragement.

As parents, other family members, friends, or as any caring person, we urge you to be strong in endorsing an unconditional status for lesbian, gay or bisexual daughters and sons in the community. This is their right. There needs to be recognition of the aroha for all which eliminates harassment and prejudice, which honours the whole being, which ensures justice both for them and for us their families.

As families we need to remember that we are entitled to a dignified place in society and that no one can take this right from us, unless we allow them the power to do so.

Most importantly, through this book and from the heartfelt contributions it contains, may you and your family be empowered and no longer be 'Invisible'.

Glossary

These definitions were compiled from a dictionary and with the help or consensus opinion of several lesbians and gay men as being generally accepted in New Zealand at this time.

AIDS
Acquired Immune Deficiency Syndrome — a profound degree of damage to the human immune system associated with infection by the Human Immunodeficiency Virus (HIV). AIDS is diagnosed by occurrence of various infections in persons with damaged immune systems.

Butch
Accentuated masculinity in men, cross-gender mannerisms in women.

Camp
Used of homosexual men and women — effeminate in mannerisms; theatrical when applied to men; becoming outdated among younger people (see Kamp).

Closet
(Contemptuous) of a secretly gay man or lesbian; now generally — secret.

Closeted
Secretly gay; 'deeply closeted' — not even 'out' or acknowledged as homosexual to oneself.

Come out
The continuing process by which a man or woman acknowledges to themselves and later family, or publicly, that they are lesbian, gay or bisexual.

Cross-dresser

Mainly used of men who like dressing in feminine clothing, in private or public May or may not be a sexual fetish Most cross dressers are not homosexual

Drag

Gender cross-dressing, mainly refers to men; hyper-feminine, especially of glamorous clothing worn by men while cross-dressing.

Drag-queen

Man who cross-dresses and/or adopts a flamboyant persona, frequently for special occasions only — often but not necessarily homosexual.

Dyke

Lesbian (not offensive unless intended so).

Faggot

Gay man (abusive); can be used by other gay men among themselves without offence.

Family

A 'code' word used by gay men or lesbians to mean 'one of us'; own gay friends or support group.

Fetish

An article which stimulates sexual desire in a susceptible person, e.g. leather, shoes, women's underwear, silk, fur or other fabrics.

Heterosexism

The prevailing and pervasive, if largely unconscious, attitude that heterosexuality is solely and compulsorily 'right and normal'; from this comes resentment and antagonism to anything which departs from this 'norm', e.g. anti-homosexual prejudice.

HIV
Human Immunodeficiency Virus (see AIDS).

Homophobia
Hatred and fear of lesbians and gay men, often subtle; homophobic — suffering from homophobia; homophobe — homophobic person.

Kamp
Used by both male and female homosexuals in NZ until the early 1970s — now generally replaced by 'gay'.

Paedophilia
Sexual condition where desire is directed at children of either sex or both; paedophile — person who displays paedophilia. (Sexual orientation and paedophilia are two distinct phenomena, independent of each other.)

Paraphilia
A condition in which a person can respond sexually only in very specific circumstances, i.e. with particular fetishes; or in discipline, bondage, sadism, masochism etc; with a particular age group, or other exact conditions.

Patriarchy
System of society, government, etc. ruled by men, to the economic, cultural and social disadvantage of women.

Pederasty
Usually used as a synonym for paedophilia.

Poof
(Poofters) — insult; sometimes used in banter among gay men — not appreciated from others.

Queen

Gay man, especially but not always with effeminate mannerisms; screaming queen — very exaggerated mannerisms. May be used by gay men mockingly of self, or by friends — not by others, which is insulting.

Queer

Abusive; now also being 'reclaimed' by some lesbians and gay men amongst themselves.

Spring

To expose the homosexual orientation or identity of another person, usually nadvertently. When done maliciously it can also be called 'Outing'.

STDs

Sexually Transmitted Diseases, e.g. Pubic Lice (crabs); Chlamydia; Genital Warts; Genital Herpes; Candida (thrush); Trichomoniasis (TV); Non-specific Vaginitis (NSV); Gonorrhoea (clap); Syphilis; Hepatitis B; HIV/AIDS.

Straight

Non-gay; a heterosexual person.

Transsexual

A person who physically and outwardly is male and who feels themself inwardly to be female, or vice versa. Some transsexuals have passed through a complete sex-change process by living entirely as their other gender identity for several years and/or by having, or intending to have, surgery to complete the process. Female/male is less frequent than male/female transsexualism.

Transvestite

A cross-dresser, usually heterosexual.

APPENDIX A

The Questionnaires and Survey

This was not a scientifically designed survey. The results apply only to the respondents, who were self-selected. The inclusion of families with transsexual or transvestite daughters or sons was not undertaken, as these were seen as special groupings which required books of their own. The author apologises to any families concerned who feel they have not been recognised here.

Totals of questionnaires received

Parents of Gay men	85
Parents of Bisexual men	4
Parents of Lesbians	23
Parents of Bisexual women	3
Family Members of Gay men	12
Family Members of Bisexual men	3
Family Members of Lesbians	7
Family Members of Bisexual women	0
Gay men	102
Bisexual men	10
Lesbians	46
Bisexual women	3
Total Respondents	298

If the total figures given in the text do not correspond, it is because a few questionnaires were received too late for inclusion in the table.

Indications of nationality were

European	247
Maori	5
Maori/European	8
Pacific Is.	1
Pacific Is/European	1
Maori/Paciflc Is.	1
Not stated	35

Distribution

The questionnaires were available for a period of just over three months from 1 June 1991 — 10 September 1991. Participation was invited as follows:

- An article by courtesy of the NZ Woman's Weekly (10 June 1991).
- An interview by courtesy of Radio NZ with Maggie Barry on National Radio, Wellington, in July 1991.
- An interview by courtesy of the Gay Broadcast Collective with Ian Kember on Access Radio, Wellington, in July 1991.
- Mail circular to some sixty lesbian, gay or other support agencies in June 1991.

These attracted 305 letters of first enquiry. It is estimated that up to 600 questionnaires were distributed — it is not possible to be exact as some groups took several copies for distribution. Photocopies were made by others, but returns of such were very few.

The second response (i.e. questionnaires completed and

returned) was 298, to which was added 12 detailed letters. This total of 310 corresponds to 100 per cent of the first enquiries, and a conservative fifty per cent of questionnaires distributed.

Such a second response was phenomenal and graphically demonstrated the need of families throughout New Zealand to be heard and recognised on these issues. It was the respondents' wish that by sharing fully of their privacy, others would become educated, informed and if possible, where applicable, spared unnecessary trauma.

The honesty of the replies was amazing and courageous. For some it was a personal 'coming out' — their effort is respected and acknowledged. Response was also received from expatriate Kiwis in Australia, Britain and Canada — their contribution is appreciated.

The author believes that although this survey is informal, it is the largest of any kind on these issues yet undertaken in New Zealand. And, while it cannot be considered entirely representative, numerically the response is significant.

Aims of questionnaires

The primary purpose was to access New Zealand parents of lesbians, gay men and bisexuals, and also their daughters, sons and other family members. It was hoped that the questions would elicit responses to show how parents and family members have reacted to their situation. Their replies showed:

- Parents are not alone, contrary to many believing they are, when they first learn that a daughter or son is lesbian, gay or bisexual

- Many parents have parallel experiences to each other, and initially react with similar thoughts and feelings

- Any negative reactions have largely been based on poor information, prejudice and homophobia

- What is happening in NZ — and not only overseas — has made parents and families feel 'invisible'

- Many parents have, by love and willingness to learn, found that new knowledge can powerfully produce a wider tolerance and deeper understanding.

It was also hoped that the responses would:

- Give an indication as to whether discrimination has declined, and if people were better informed five years after the Homosexual Law Reform Act (1986)

- Indicate any discrimination still being experienced by lesbian, gay or bisexual daughters and sons, from families and/or from society at large

- Give an indication of attempted, considered, or completed suicide due to homophobic pressures and the experience of being lesbian, gay or bisexual

- Show how siblings and other family members were feeling and reacting to their family situation and to the issues involved

- How daughters and sons were feeling about themselves, their parents and families, what support they needed, and what support they had/had not received.

Collation of the questionnaire responses was honestly and carefully attempted. It was an enormous task, as each had some twenty three questions, and respondents frequently elaborated on separate sheets of paper. As the survey was informal, these statistics are not for general publication (to avoid extrapolation into other works, as this would not be appropriate or desirable). As promised to respondents, every personal letter and questionnaire has been destroyed.

APPENDIX B

Maori and Polynesian Lesbians and Gay Men

Maori Homosexuality

There were only a few identifiably Maori responses to the questionnaires, so that it was not possible to gain a wholly representative perspective from the survey. Nor was I able to make personal contact with Maori parents. As well, some Maori lesbians and gay men felt that, as tangata whenua (the indigenous people of the land), it is for them to speak or to write about themselves. I respect this point of view. The following quotes are from responses to the questionnaires:

A Lesbian Daughter Says:

'Growing up in two cultures (my family adopted the Maori way) has made being lesbian another life challenge which has been right for me with all its "good, bad, and ugly" bits in it. As with anything in life, whatever path you want, just walk it, and give it your best. I must admit that all through my life I've believed deeply in my cultural Aroha (love), where Wairua (spirit) — which is confined to no forms of religion, nor excluded from it — is the root and record of me being a Person, a Maori, and a Lesbian. I am not aware of any Kaumatua (elders) who openly reject us, because when we are all together on the marae (tribal meeting place), we're there as one unit. Wairua, Mana (personal prestige) and Aroha have preference over everything else.'

A Gay Son Explains:

'I am Ngati Kahungunu. When I look in the mirror I see a Maori; when I'm on the marae I am Maori; when I'm with my Maori network I am Maori; but for the remaining eighty per cent of the time I am a gay individual.

'To those gays and lesbians thinking of "coming out" (a term which I hate!), it's okay to be scared or frightened. The feelings of loneliness, or frustration, and about AIDS can create a heavy burden on your shoulders. Speaking for myself, even though I was ninety-nine per cent certain I would be okay, the other one per cent sure felt a lot heavier. All I can say is you'll know when you're ready. Not your family or best friend or counsellor — but YOU. When it is something or someone else other than your heart — then it's wrong for you.'

This contributor also says, 'When I told my parents Mum started crying. She was blaming herself saying that she had "smothered" me in my early teen years. She was frightened about AIDS, gay bashings, the outside world. I just hugged her. I felt like for once — I could be ME in front of my family. Yes, occasionally I might think "why am I not heterosexual like my other friends?" but I snap out of it.'

Knowing that many families are united across races, and that the Maori experience is generally of interest to New Zealanders, I searched other writings in an effort to gain further insight. This passage is taken from *Mana Wahine Maori* by Ngahuia Te Awekotuku:

'We are the inheritors of a Polynesian tradition of the Mahu of Hawaii, Tahiti, the Cook Islands, the Marquesas; of the Fa'afafine of Samoa, of the Fakaleiti of Tonga, of the Carmens and Shirelles and Natashas of Aotearoa (New Zealand) ... Yet we do not have a common, everyday name for us ... we do have one word, takatapui. And, ironically, this word is associated with one of the most romantic, glamorised, man / woman love stories of the Maori world, the leg-

end of Hinemoa and Tutanekai. Tutanekai with his flute and favourite intimate friend, his hoa takatapui (intimate same-gender friend), Tiki . . .

'... Of women, though, there is even less on record, yet we did exist. The story of Wairaka tells us about the woman who, in saving the canoe Mataatua with her superb strength, named a locality and said "Kia whakatane au i hau. Let me be as strong as the strongest man." ... Her unlucky demise, pairing off under pressure with a man, tells us even more. And her journey north to settle here in this district (Auckland), on the isthmus with her supporters, most of them women, away from her husband, tells us something very special. For Owairaka, the place of Wairaka, remembers her ... Indeed, the loving of one's own gender is an ancient, even tribal practice, honourable and revered.'

As background information, Phil Parkinson, honorary curator of the Lesbian and Gay Archives of NZ, wrote in an article for the Second ILGA Pink Book (1988):

'We know little of homosexuality among Maori people before colonisation. The missionaries, for the most part, were unaware of it, seeing Maori culture through their own cultural perspectives. But Richard Davis observed that same sex unions in adolescence were common, and marriages were sometimes seen. Similar traditions survive in Polynesian cultures in Samoa and Tonga to this day ...'

And in Parker & Hulme — A Lesbian View Julie Glamuzina and Alison Laurie commented:

'In pre-European Maori societies same-sex relationships seem to have been a part of ordinary life. The 1988 Royal Commission on Social Policy noted that: "Of specific concern to Maori lesbians ... is the claim ... that homosexuality

was introduced by Pakeha (European) and that it had no place in traditional Maori society.

'There is no evidence to support this claim. Kuia and kaumatua (female and male elders) have suggested to the Commission that on the contrary homosexuality — male and female — was not uncommon in pre-European times and that it was in fact more readily accepted than today.'

The accounts given here, although sparse, will I hope help others wishing to further search for information.

Polynesian Homosexuality

Although many Pacific Island communities are racially represented in New Zealand, it was not possible for me to research the issues of being gay, lesbian or bisexual from all of these, as I was limited by lack of contacts, resources and time factors.

In 1992 The Pacific Islands AIDS Trust published its own handbook for AIDS prevention, education and training. In it, representatives of Samoa, Cook Islands, Tokelau, Niue, Fiji and Tonga appealed strongly for a dedication to the preservation of 'our heritage, the family, And for all those suffering from AIDS'.

This handbook is easily read, being largely in Pacific Island languages as well as in English, and has colourful illustrations. In the foreword, T. Louisa Crawley (Chairperson of the Trust) says:

'The main focus of the programme is THE FAMILY, therefore, the planning and development of the programme needed to take into account the most culturally appropriate methods and language to communicate the information, clearly and sensitively to our communities.'

In her concluding remarks she calls for a conscious striving for the total eradication of HIV/AIDS, which is a threat to the Pacific peoples' heritage and their families.

Western Samoan Gays /Mala in New Zealand

As Western Samoa is the largest of the Pacific Island communities in New Zealand today, I felt Samoans required some recognition in a book about New Zealand issues of homosexuality. Despite enquiries, it was not possible for me to ascertain any reference to lesbianism in the Western Samoan community, and I am grateful to Karl Pulotu-Endemann, a founder-member of the Pacific Islands AIDS Trust who is active in health and education for all Pacific Islanders in New Zealand, for his help. As a Western Samoan living in New Zealand since boyhood, yet closely aligned to his heritage, he has kindly allowed me to use the following extracts from studies being prepared for future publication, as his personal contribution. The histories quoted are taken from both formal and informal interviews he has made. In this statement on 'Fa'afafine — Gays in Western Samoan Culture in New Zealand' he explains:

> *'The Samoan name for effeminate males is fa'afafine which literally means "like a woman ". Fa 'afafine also encompasses homosexual or gay males who may not dress in "drag" or female clothing or be effeminate. In the mid-1960s amongst fa;'afafine gays there was a deliberate move to adopt the term "mala" rather than fa'afafine. Although the term "mala" derives from the word "malaia" ("a burden" or being cursed), in the context used by Samoan gays in referring to each other it loses any negativity.'*

Interviewed respondents said:

'I've always been a mala. I've never known anything else. Growing up in Samoa you get to know about sex very early on, especially amongst the boys. We used to play and sleep with the other boys in our village.'

'I came from a village where my parents had a prominent role in the church and although they accepted me, I went to Apia [the capital of Western Samoa] to get away.'

'Growing up in Samoa I never had to "come out of the closet" like some of my palagi [European] friends. Everybody knew I was gay.'

'I came from a family of fourteen boys, my mother gave me all the jobs that a girl would do like cooking and cleaning. I also tended to mix with girls and after a while it became known that I was fa'afafine, but it was never a negative thing. It was just part of my life.'

It was apparent from the interviews that growing up gay in Samoa in the 1960s and 1970s was different from the 1980s and 1990s:

'I have just come back from Samoa,' says a forty-eight-year-old Samoan mala. 'I can't believe the number of mala in Apia, particularly young ones. They are so outrageous compared to us when we were that age.'

'When I was at school in Samoa in the seventies there were many mala in my class and some in the lower grades. The thing that stands out now is the number of young mala — some as young as ten years old and their outrageous behaviour.'

At school in Samoa the mala tend to be more acceptable to other pupils and to teachers than in New Zealand:

'I came to New Zealand when nine years old in the 1950s. Always knowing I was gay it was no big thing until I came here. My parents, particularly my mother, tried to make me walk more manly and talk in a lower voice — but it never worked. Mum believed it would lessen the ridicule. The worst period and yet the most precious was when I was at High School. During this time I realised how strong I was in fighting the ridicule and prejudice of pupils and some teachers. There was at the same time tremendous support from school friends and particularly some female teachers. To counteract the "negativeness" received from the name-calling of "homo" and other snide remarks, I consciously made an effort to excel in my studies.'

'When I was at a high school for boys, being half Samoan made me stand out. Being gay was something you didn't talk about. It was interesting that although there was a "macho all rugby culture" I knew quite a few gay pupils and teachers. When a headmaster later announced intentions of interviewing all teachers to ascertain their sexuality, because he would not tolerate any gay teachers in his school, I laughed. I mean it's happening all around him.'

Despite discriminatory actions they'd experienced being both Samoan and gay, respondents stated that from their viewpoint being Samoan and gay was also the most positive thing about them — giving personal support and strength.

'Being Samoan and being mala is not a handicap, but a strength.'

'We all come from an aiga [family] and being a Samoan mala also means that we belong to a special aiga.'

'If Samoan mala can survive the anti-gay and anti-Samoan influences of the church, the education system and in some cases the anti-gay sentiments of their own family, then I believe we are very strong people.'

At TVNZ in Auckland I spoke with Susana Hukui who hosts the programme 'Tagata Pasifika'. She showed me a video of a programme she had facilitated on AIDS and the Pacific Island community's response. The programme featured Karl Pulotu-Endemann speaking on behalf of the Pacific Islands AIDS Trust, of which he is a founder-member. He said:

> *'The churches need to be facilitating open discussion. At present the rigid belief that to be homosexual is a sin against oneself and against God is not helping our young people. Many of us hold a stern disapproval of homosexual people, a narrow belief that all sexual expression by them is casual, and that to use condoms is wrong.'*

Selected Further Reading

This reading list is a guide only. It contains a selection from the background reading for this book, which could not be an exhaustive research. For those who wish to read more widely or pursue particular topics, most of the titles listed here have useful bibliographies.

Gay/Lesbian/Bisexual Lives and Theory

Awekotuku, Ngahuia Te (1991) *Mana Wahine Maori*, New Women's Press, NZ; (1988) *Bisexual Lives*, Off Pink Publishing, London. (personal experiences)

Bauer, Marion Dane, ed (1994) *Am I Blue? Coming Out From the Silence*, New York (fiction)

Cowan, Thomas (1988) *Gay Men and Women Who Enriched the World*, William Mulvey Inc., USA.

Duberman, M.B., M. Vicinus, and G. Chauncey (1989) *Hidden from History: reclaiming Gay and Lesbian past*, New American Library, Penguin Books, USA.

Faderman, Lillian (1985) *Surpassing the Love of Men*, The Women's Press, UK (lesbian history)

Glamuzina, Julie and Alison J. Laurie (1991) *Parker & Hulme — A Lesbian View*, New Women's Press, NZ.

Grahn,Judy (1990) *Another Mother Tongue: Gay Words, Gay Worlds*, Boston.

Hall Carpenter Archives (1989), Gay Men's Oral History Group, *Walking After Midnight — Gay Men's Life Stories*, Routledge, USA.

Heart, Mikaya (1994), *The Straight Woman's Guide to Lesbianism*, California.

Hutchins, Loraine, and Lani, Kaahumanu, eds (1991) *Bi Any Other Name: Bisexual People Speak Out*, London.

Katz, Jonathan Ned (1990) *Gay/Lesbian Almanac — A New Documentary*, Harper & Row, USA.

Lesbian History Group (1989) *Not a Passing Phase*, The Women's Press, UK.

McEwen, Christine and Sue O'Sullivan, eds (1988) *Out the Other Side — Contemporary Lesbian Writing*, Virago Press, UK. (personal experiences)

Oikawa, Mona, Dionne Falconer, Ann Dector, eds (1994) *Resist! Essays*

Against a Homophobic Culture, Canada.

Penelope, Julia and Susan J. Wolfe, eds (expanded edition1989) *The Original Coming Out Stories*, The Crossing Press, USA. (personal experiences)

Rich, Adrienne (1980), *Compulsory Heterosexuality and Lesbian Existence*, SIGNS Vol 5, No.4, USA.

Trenchard, Lorraine (1989), *Being Lesbian*, GMP Publishers (a guide and explanation)

HIV/AIDS

Brown, Rebecca (1995) *The Gifts of the Body*, New York (fiction).

Dilley, James W, Cheri Pies and Michael Helquist (1989) *Face to Face — A Guide to AIDS Counselling*, AIDS Health Project, Celestial Arts, USA (mainly for therapists).

Holloway, Trish (1993) *My Friend Bo and Me* (for children) and *But What if they ask Me?* (for teachers and parents) sold as a set of two, Whangarei Education Resource Centre, NZ. Available from P.O. Box 1813, Whangarei New Zealand.

Pearson, Carol Wynn (1986) *Goodbye, I Love You*, Columbus Books, UK (a wife's coming to terms with a husband's homosexuality and later AIDS).

Rodale, Ardath H. (1989) *Climbing Towards the Light*, Rodale Press, USA. (a mother's account of a gay son, and his eventual HIV/AIDS)

Taylor, Ray, Trish Gribben et al (1989) *Living With HIV— A Personal Handbook*, N.Z. AIDS Foundation.

'The Authors' (1992) *A.I.D.S Education Prevention Training Programme*, Pacific Islands A.I.D.S Trust.

Homosexual Relationships

Berzon, Betty (1990) *Permanent Partners*, Plume Penguin (lesbian and gay).

Berzon, Betty, ed. (1992) *Positively Gay*, Celestial Arts, USA (lesbian and gay).

McWhirter, David P. and Andrew M. Mattinson (1984) *The Male Couple*, Prentice-Hall, USA (written pre-AIDS).

Law

Auckland Lesbian and Gay Lawyers Group (1994) *Out Law: A Legal Guide for Lesbians and Gay Men in New Zealand*, Auckland.

Parkinson, Phil (1989) *Sexual Law Reform — the NZ Experience from Wolfenden until the Crimes Bill*, Lesbian & Gay Archives of New Zealand.

Pharr, Suzanne (1988) *Homophobia: A Weapon of Sexism*, Arizona.

Parents

Abbott, Dr. Max (1985) *Homosexuality — An Overview of Research and Professional Opinion*, Mental Health Foundation of New Zealand.

Borhek, Mary V. (1983) *Coming Out to Parents*, The Pilgrim Press, USA.

Borhek, Mary V. (1979) *My Son Eric*, The Pilgrim Press, USA

Clark, Don (1987) *The New Loving Someone Gay*, Celestial Arts, U.S.A.

Donnelly, Felix (1984) *Flames and Ether*, Allen & Unwin/Port Nicholson Press, NZ.

Donnelly, Felix (1989) *Teenage Sexuality: New Zealand Parents' Guide*, G.P. Books, NZ.

Griffen, C.W., M.J. Wirth and A.G. Wirth (1986) *Beyond Acceptance*, St Martin's Press,USA

Guss Back, Gloria (1985) *Are You Still My Mother?* Warner Books, USA.

Collective Gay Information, ed. (1982) *'Official Findings and Recommendations'*, New South Wales Anti-Discrimination Board Report on Homosexuality, Australia.

Rafkin, Louise, ed. (1987) *Different Daughters*, Cleis Press, USA.

Silverstein, Dr Charles (1977) *A Family Matter — a Parents' Guide to Homosexuality*, McGraw-Hill, USA.

Religion

Bromell, David, Felix Donnelly, William Hem, Rosemary Neave (1991) *Love Unbounded — on being Gay or Lesbian and Christian*, Colcom Press, NZ.

Lewis, J.J., Allan Davidson et al (1991) *Homosexuality: Christian Perspective*, Colcom Press, NZ.

Spong, Bishop John Shelby (1988) *Living in Sin? — a Bishop Rethinks Human Sexuality*, Harper & Row, USA.

Spong, Bishop John Shelby (1991) *Rescuing the Bible from Fundamentalism*, Harper Collins, USA.

Veritas Group (1985) *Scripture & Homosexuality — a guide to the perplexed Parliamentarian*, Wellington, NZ.

Sexology/ Psychology/ Sociology

Bernstein, Barbara (1990) 'Attitudes and Issues of Parents of Gay Men and Lesbians and Implications for Therapy', *Journal of Gay & Lesbian Psychotherapy*, Vol. 1 (3), The Haworth Press Inc., USA.

Bozett, Frederick W., ed. (1989) *Homosexuality and the Family*, The Harrington Press Inc., USA.

Durden-Smith, Jo and Diane Desimone (1983) *Sex and the Brain*, Arbor House, USA.

Moir, Anne and David Jessel (1989) *Brain Sex*, Michael Joseph Ltd, UK.

Money, John (1990) *Gay, Straight and Inbetween*, Oxford University Press,

USA.
Reiter, Laura M., ed. (1989) 'Sexual Orientation, Sexual Identity and the Question of Choice', CISW report in *Clinical Social Work Journal*, Vol. 17 (2) Summer, Human Sciences Press.
Weeks, Jeffrey (1986) *Sexuality*, Ellis Horwood Limited & Tavistock Publications Limited, UK.
Weinburg, Dr. George (1972) *Society and the Healthy Homosexual*, St Martin's Press, USA.
Weinrich, James D. (1987) *Sexual Landscapes*, Macmillan, USA.

Support

Borysenko,Joan (1990), *Guilt is the Teacher, Love is the Lesson*, Warner Books Inc., USA.
Haines, Hilary (1987) *Mental Health for Women*, Reed Methuen, NZ.
Hanson, Dr. Peter (1988), *The Joy of Stress — How to make pressure work for you*, Pan Books, UK (applicable to many situations).
Jeffers, Susan (1987) *Feel the Fear And Do It Anyway*, Century Hutchinson, UK. (applicable to many situations).
King, Petrea (1988) *Quest for Life — A Holistic Approach to Life-Threatening Diseases*, Equinox Publishing, The Craftsman's Press, Australia (cancer and HIV/AIDS).
Needham, Gwen (1991) *High Roads — Keys to Personal Power*, Power-Principle Publications. Available from G. Needham, R.D. 2, Hikurangi, Northland, N.Z.

Youth

Bauer, Marion Dane, ed (1994) *Am I Blue? Coming Out From the Silence*, New York (fiction)
Department of Health (March 1990) *Adolescent Sexuality*, Taskforce Report, NZ.
Gibson, Paul (1989) *Youth Suicide — report on the Secretary's Task Force*, U.S. Department of Health & Human Services.
Rampton, Leigh, and Paul Kinder (1991) *Finding Out —A Resource Kit for Professional, Workers with Youth & Counsellors*, N.Z. AIDS Foundation (includes pamphlets & posters, available from Foundation).
Taylor, Barry co-ord. (1989) *Gay and Lesbian Youth Services in N.Z. — discussion paper*, Youth Mental Health Project.
Taylor, William (1994) *The Blue Lawn*, Auckland (fiction).

CPSIA information can be obtained at www.ICGtesting.com
Printed in the USA
LVOW011658220911

247434LV00018B/72/P

9 780980 552300